For Mom.

THE FEAST
OF THE SEVEN FISHES
A BROOKLYN ITALIAN'S RECIPES
CELEBRATING FOOD & FAMILY

By Daniel Paterna

 powerHouse Books BROOKLYN, N.Y.

FOREWORD

By Michael Lomonaco

Feast of the Seven Fishes: A Brooklyn Italian's Recipes Celebrating Food and Family reads as though it came from my own family's kitchen. The narrative is much like my own family history, and the food as if it came from my own mother's kitchen. Daniel Paterna's vibrant stories and delicious, authentic recipes make for one great read, and an even better outing in the kitchen. Cooking the holiday classics of the Feast of the Seven Fishes and the Christmas Eve feast, or the everyday pasta and beans will be an evocative experience—an authentic look into the Italian American world that is quickly fading from view. I feel so at home here. You will too as you read it, enjoy the photos, and cook the recipes.

The photographs are an insightful view into the lives of generations of Brooklyn Italian families, and tell the story completely and clearly. I know these not-so-mean streets and their friendly and generous purveyors of fine foods, which filled the larder of every family I knew in my younger days. The portraits, street view, and kitchen shots moved me deeply. Maybe because I shopped in these markets and grew up learning about food in these same shops. I learned to love food in the very places that Daniel did, and I have the same love and respect for many of those shown here.

This deeply personal book is meant to move you, to help you understand the story of one family, and to see that so many other families lived much like this.

From the photographs to the recipes, and from the family history to the people, this book weaves a story that is familiar, yet still lyrical and magical. Inviting you into his family's home, Paterna shares the warmth and love that his mother, Anne, would want you to feel.

I knew Anne. I worked with her at a neighborhood bank where, as a college student, I had my first grown-up job as a part-time bank teller. Anne trained and supervised me and remained a friend from the neighborhood for life. Anne was warm and welcoming, quick to smile and laugh, and even quicker to share a delicious home-cooked treat, like arancini. She passed so many of her traits on to Daniel, and I am especially gladdened that she gave him a love for food and family—and her recipe book, as well.

Every immigrant group brings its former way of life with them, adapting to the myriad differences they find in the American landscape and the stark reality that here is not there. The foods, clothing, language, and religious differences are shaped to fit this new world, while maintaining as much of the old world as possible. As the son of Sicilian immigrants I can attest to my personal experiences and the way my own family adapted to the American lifestyle. My father arrived in 1924, and his assimilation story is like many of his generation. The Italian American story is as unique as every other immigrant tale, yet the same: poverty, outsider status, striving to succeed against all odds. The story of our ancestral struggles was often told at the dining table, where we heard so much of this history at Sunday dinners, recounted with laughter and tears. What we ate is seen so clearly in this book: a veritable community recipe book of the Italian American dishes that accompanied those stories, which were passed from the elders to their younger, native-born American children.

As the torch is passed on to the next generation, so too are the tales, myths, and dreams of the elders, and the foods we ate. So now, with them here in your hand, I encourage you to cook for someone you love and share this story with them, because in the end we are all the same—our shared experiences and common ground all grown from the same seed.

INTRODUCTION

My mom's go-to meal planner: a treasure chest of recipes

Stuffed Escarole

Filling — pine raisins pignoli garlic capers
use green chopped green & black olives
sparingly & anchovies (—————)

In pan put oil + garlic — sauté for
a few minutes then place escarole — til
done.   1 can anchovies
                 escarole

---

3 lamb shanks
cut 1" size   4 cup celery
Boil lamb in some water + put
celery & onions.
When that's cooked add boiled
chickory to it (squeeze water out
of chickory + cut it into small pieces
with scissors. When ready to
eat scramble 3 eggs add cheese

Crabs

(illegible mixed notes — crabs, garlic, brown, hot pepper, chopped parsley, add tomatoes let cook for ½ hr, then add paste, last 45 min add crabs)

Stuffed Squid

get at least 6 lb cleaned — get larger size
stuffing before put pignoli in sauce
2 or 3 egg yolks   take them out at
          plenty of grated cheese
          pignoli + raisins   use quite a
          garlic + parsley   bit of bread
          salt + black pepper

Sea Salad for (4)

2 LBS. OCTOPUS — buy small
1 LB. LOBSTER TAILS
1/2 LB. SCUNGELLI — use more chopped garlic
2 1/4 lb SHRIMP — 2 lbs
1 1/2 LBS. SQUID ...PEEL SKIN OFF BEFORE BOILING

*MARINATE SEA SALAD 1 DAY BEFORE .. ONLY GARLIC
DAY OF ADD CELERY - PEPPER - LEMON - OLIVE OIL - PEPPER
for more then 5 people
FRESH PARSLEY (chopped)

OCTOPUS GRAVEY - FOR 3 LBS. OF MACARONI BUY 6 lbs.
OF OCTOPUS   remove only skin off
BUY LARGE OCTAPUS   the head   receipe
FOR SAUCE   see octopus card

---

1 doz Struffoli + some white   3 lb honey
                               need doz eggs yolks
3 egg yolks — beat very well
or less tea of baking powder
3 tsps. baking powder   full flour
(anisette   half wine glass) let stay in
 tangerine) skin cut fine)   stove for
                               a while cook

Throw in eggs — beat again
Put enough flour on egg batter until
you can knead it — about 1 lb 3/4
first (melt honey)   use some water

Ravioli

1 1/2 flour
2 eggs
luke-warm water
(oil)

filling
2 eggs
butter
cheese
parsley

Manicotti

2 full flour
3-4 eggs — oil
cold water

boil mac. for
5 minutes
scoop out each
(—) 2 at a time

OCTOPUS SAUCE

4 LBS. OCTOPUS ...USE (3) CANS TOMATO &
                       (1) PASTE

AT XMAS BUY 6 LBS OCTOPUS USE REDPACK &
                                         PASTE

PEEL SKIN OFF THE HEAD OF OCTOPUS

4 laddles of sauce for 1 lb.
                        linguine
6 lbs octopus for more than 5 people
2 1/2 to 3 lbs paste   over

Puttanesca

1 small can (—) anchovies + black olives
1 can or 1 large can tomato no paste
                                + anchovies
brown garlic & anchovies
add some olives while cooking
when sauce is cooked & mac
being served put some anchovies
on top of mac to dress it up
(2 small cans tomato) — 1 1/2 lbs mac

This is not a cookbook in the classic sense. It is a visual history of my family's cooking traditions and of my connections to my Italian American heritage. It is an exploration of the cultural DNA that links events, times, and traditions together. I've tried to portray the simple meals my family shared in an elevated light. It is an account of the culinary heritage of millions Italian immigrants, and the dishes our ancestors brought with them on their journey to the New World. It is the simple meals my family shared in an elevated light.

Most immigrant traditions will yield to the American way of life. I remember my grandmother preparing Italian meals downstairs while upstairs, my mom might be preparing a 1960s space-age-style meal out of a box. Sitting at my grandmother's cloth-covered table, I sensed how much she relished the joy I found in her food, and after dinner, she would show me postcards from family and friends in Naples, and provide a heartfelt narration of the Italy she so missed.

Today, gathering around a dinner table with family or friends can seem like a burden or a scheduling nightmare. I feel challenged by these pressures in my own second-generation Italian American experience. But the continuity represented by these recipes shows how important it is to sit for a meal as a family—celebrating togetherness as a life-sustaining gift.

This is a visual archive of generations who had their full share of challenges, balancing work and life, the old and the new. As the older generation fades away, I feel as though I am at the delta of my family's culinary river, catching as much as I can to keep it from drifting away.

These recipes are grounded in the everyday experience of the people that inhabited my childhood: the denizens of Bensonhurst. The children and grandchildren of a distant country that still kept its hold on them. These recipes are part of their life stories and their legacy. The first part is a personal account of these people and of the stories they told around the dinner table.

The second part introduces some of the shopkeepers of Bensonhurst: bakers, fishmongers, pasta makers. The purveyors of many of the tools and ingredients required to create the meals of my childhood. In this section, there are recipes inspired by each of these shops.

The heart of the book is dedicated to the foods my family prepared on special holidays. Each section is organized around the sequence of dishes that are traditionally served on the day. Visual memory helped me recreate these dishes as I remember them, and I tried to locate and use many of the plates and platters my parents and grandparents passed around our table. I close with a selection of dishes that will turn any day into a holiday.

All of the photographs were taken on low-light film, mostly using unbalanced and natural light or the General Electric movie light my father used on his Revere 8mm camera. I used analog lenses on the handful of images taken on a digital camera to maintain visual consistency and to evoke the ambience of these festive meals.

Opposite page: My mother's original recipe cards: masterpieces of the art of process

My Parents

My parents, Anne and James, on their wedding day, May 19, 1951

Parents and grandparents often pass from this earth taking their stories, traditions, and recipes with them.

The birthright of every young person is to embrace the new. In my own adolescence, I rebelled against the very institutions of which I so fondly write. A parent myself, I quietly weather my chidren's rebellious onslaught as my parents did mine. My profound hope is that these traditions become the best part of their own family.

It is true that she challenged the stereotype of the Italian American mom in a housedress. My mother had four careers: mother, bank teller of 30 years, seamstress, and alto vocalist at her local church. She often said, "I don't know how I did it." However, my mother also had an unrecognized career as a curator of recipes and preserver of traditions. Anne took it upon herself to make sure certain recipes didn't get lost in an increasingly fast-food world. Her mission was simple, although the process was not: To translate all of the pinches, handfuls, and approximate timings into actual measures, minutes, and processes. She typed these recipes on index cards, making careful revisions whenever a friend or relative suggested a change. The art and patina of these evolving notations has always been a great source of inspiration and comfort.

Mom, Brooklyn, 1958. Taken by my dad on 8mm film.

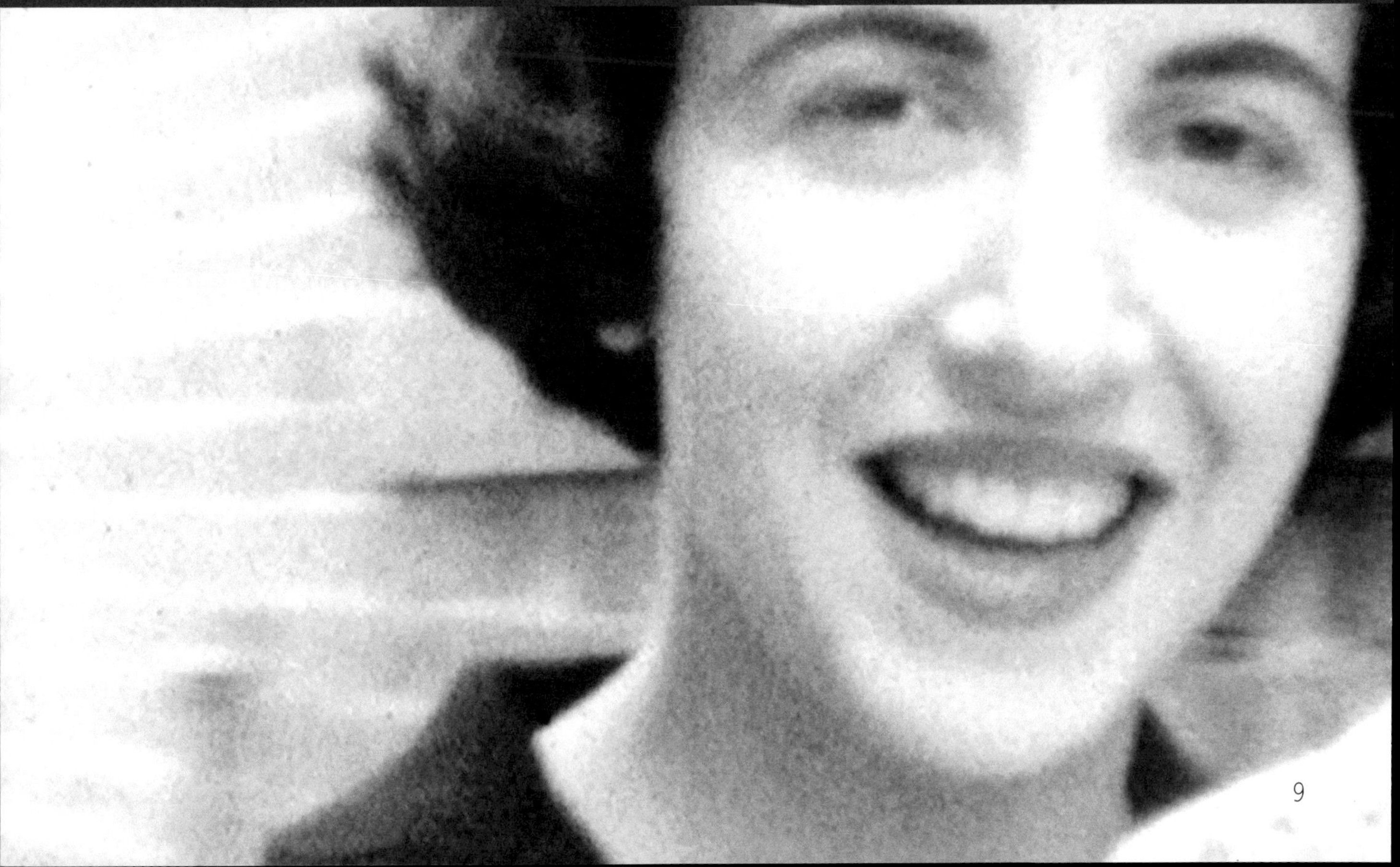

Left to right: Me, my brother, and our dad on our annual vacation to Valley Dairy Farm, Newburgh, New York, 1962

A story from my youth: The setting is an unlikely location. My father and I are at Dyker Beach Golf Course, a place where Tiger Woods' own father played on any given day.

One Saturday morning, after waking me from my adolescent slumber at the ungodly hour of 8:00 a.m. my father asked if I wanted a "cucuzielli and eggs" (a zucchini frittata panino). Like most sleepy teenagers at that age, I replied curtly, "N-O, no!" My father gave up on culinary enlightenment that morning and we went on our way to play 18 holes of beginner golf. Definition of beginner golf: Trying to hit a one-and-a-half-inch ball using a two-by-three-inch club face attached to a three-and-a-half-foot club. Hauling 30 pounds of golf clubs through marsh, muck, grass, and sand in 90-degree heat for four miles inspired lots of personal reflection, especially as players behind us yelled, "Play faster!" Around the 12th hole, my dad pulled a lunch sack from his golf bag, unwrapped his panino and began to eat joyfully. I watched silently with hungry eyes. After a moment, he tossed a sandwich to me. He smiled as I caught it. I smiled as I bit into it. It was delicious.

That lunch, and other meals like it, taught me the central influence of my stomach. It taught me to be attuned to my meal clock, and I learned to plan ahead before the hunger crash. In my own experience as a father, I think of that sandwich when my son, despite having said "no," grins with simple pleasure as he unpacks the lunch made for him.

There were many awakening moments at everyday meals and family gatherings. However, I mainly learned as I stood by my mother's side in our Bensonhurst kitchen as she prepared the family dinner. Working next to my mother, I took mental and sensory notes, and in the process, honed my own culinary skills. In later years, I would call her at home to check the ingredients for a sauce, or simply to refresh my impressionistic memory of a memorable dish.

As a parent myself, I was thrilled to share what I had learned with my own children, Luca and Madeline.

From their very early years, I would perch Luca and Madeline on the counter to either side of me while I cooked. It was a fun game in which they got to assist me, and to taste the results of their labor. Eventually they learned the processes of food preparation, but also the yearly cycles of family events, birthdays, and holidays requiring special meals. It is reassuring for me to see that the idea of meals and planning has become part of their daily lives even as they get ready to leave for college. I look forward to answering their phone calls and questions, as my mom did mine.

My daughter Madeline, aged 6, helping knead the dough for Easter bread

My Grandparents

My maternal grandparents' beautiful passports

My grandmother, Luigia (Louisa) Starace, was born in 1890 in Vico Equense, Italy, three years after Lady Liberty was erected in New York Harbor. Louisa met my grandfather, Pasquale Pastore at a candy store on Van Brunt Street in Red Hook, Brooklyn, around 1915. When she was forced to return to Italy, my grandfather promised that he would bring her back to America as his bride when the time was right. He stayed behind, mastering his trade as a tailor at Wanamaker's in Manhattan, as well learning French and English. He finally proposed to Louisa by letter 10 years after their initial meeting in the candy store.

Louisa, back in the village of Vico Equense, needed to enlist her niece Giuseppina to write letters and ultimately translate Pasquale's proposal, for she was illiterate even in Italian. My grandparents married in 1925 and after their honeymoon, they never returned to Italy. Louisa and Giuseppina reunited 35 years later.

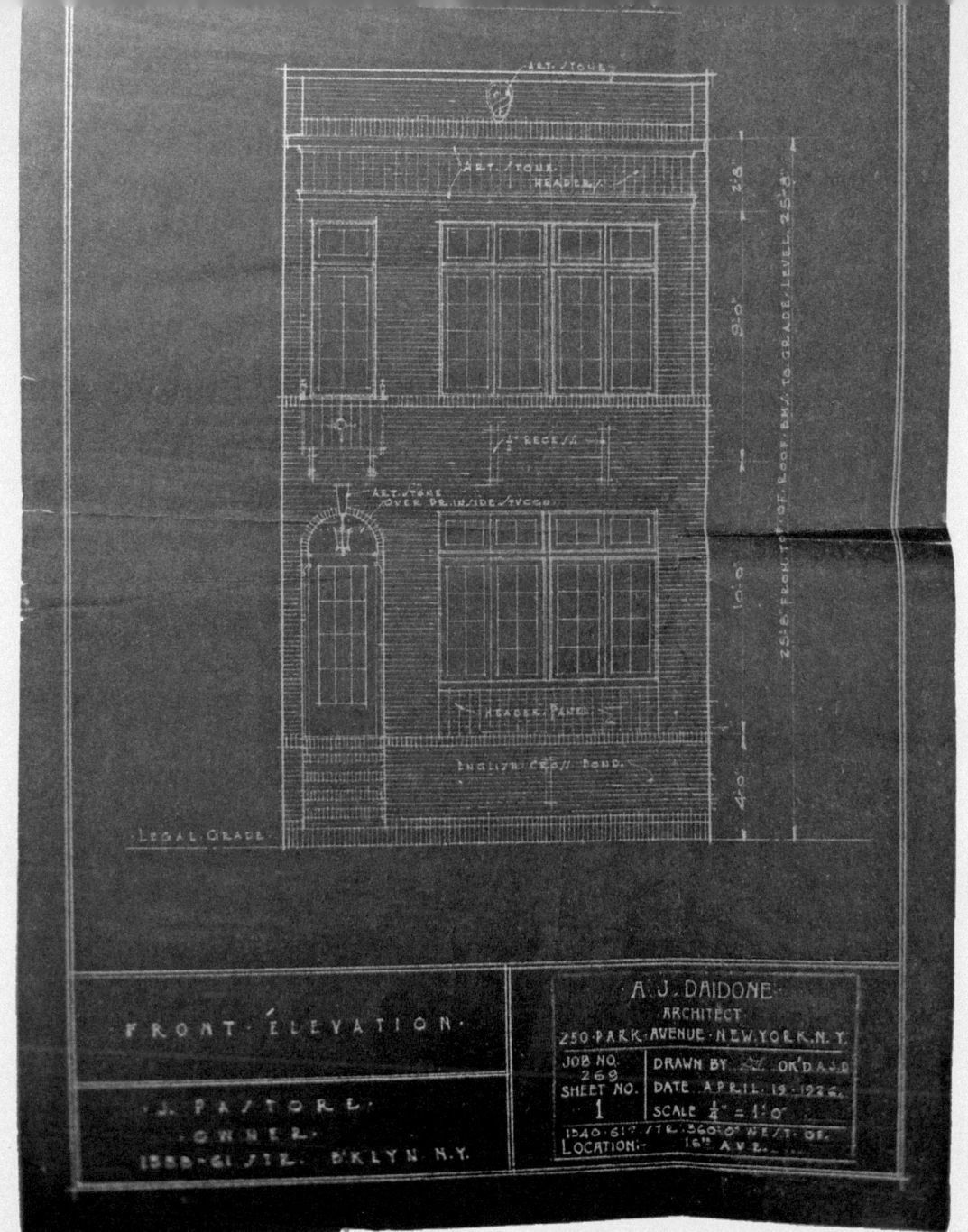

Blueprint of the house my grandfather had built on 61st Street, Brooklyn

Back in Brooklyn, my grandfather began a project of love. He purchased a plot of land at 1542 61st Street, in the northern reaches of Bensonhurst, and began building a red-brick house. My grandparents moved into their new house in 1926. Eventually the house would be divided into two separate apartments. Our family lived on the top floor, and my grandparents lived in the downstairs apartment. They would spend the rest of their days there. My mother, born at the same address, would live her entire life at 1542 61st Street. My brother, Robert, and I were also born there, and continue to be the proud guardians of our Brooklyn legacy.

I first visited Vico Equense in 1993. As I walked around the town, I saw reflections of my grandmother in the faces of the townspeople. I remembered her leaning towards our Brooklyn alleyway breeze, and realized what she had imagined. I felt the breeze drifting off the Bay of Naples, where once she dove for coins flipped overboard by tourists on cruise ships. She seemed to return to me as I stood by those shores. It was then I began to see my grandparents as immigrants before they were my family.

Not until I experienced Rome, and then traveled further south, did I begin to understand my own inner rhythms. Reconnecting to my grandmother and her melodic dialect taught me how to express what was trapped in the back of my voice. Enrolling in conversational Italian only endeared me more to the Neapolitan dialect, best heard in the 1992 movie *Ciao, Professore!* This endearing portrayal revealed a spiritual connection between the street-smart children of Naples and my own Brooklyn childhood.

My grandmother's postcard of the main piazza in Vico Equense. I stood in the same spot a century later.

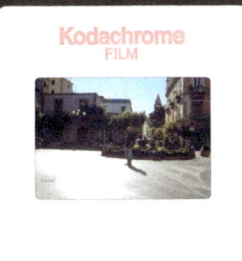

Top: Pasquale, Louisa, and their three daughters (my mom, center).
Above: Kodachromes of me in Piazza Umberto and the beach my grandmother so fondly spoke of

Louisa's tambourine, circa 1900. One the few possessions she brought from Italy.

My grandmother never felt truly at home in the U.S. Her limited English and lack of education weighed on her confidence. Yet sometimes, when she played tambourine and sang, my grandmother would reveal a glimpse of her unbroken spirit. Her youthful self emerged from the role I had assigned her—my senior citizen grandma—and I saw a glimpse of the young girl in the Red Hook candy shop.

My grandfather's proficiency as a fine tailor, his command of three languages, and his modest education gave him the confidence to become my grandmother's bridge to Brooklyn, when he became a citizen. His death in 1956 left her with three daughters and a sense of being exposed, somehow misplaced, here in their brave new world.

Despite being a naturalized citizen, my grandmother still harbored a fear of officials and hid beneath our basement steps whenever census takers arrived at the house. Maybe she was worried about being viewed as a religious minority or a "pagan worshipper." The Southern Italian parade of saints in the streets during feast days was not the accepted norm. Immigrants might be perceived as anarchists or even terrorists. I sometimes wonder what Louisa would make of our current political climate in America. She would be worried about the rhetoric of hate and intolerance. I am convinced Louisa would be the first to offer sanctuary to all immigrants, if she were alive today.

My grandmother, Louisa, during what would be her final trip to Italy, sitting in a rowboat she would have used in Vico Equense

Bensonhurst and Beyond

Kids on 18th Avenue, Brooklyn, 1970

Growing up in Bensonhurst, we learned about nutrition, not from the newest fads, but from our parents, aunts, uncles, neighbors, and grandparents. Yes, there was plenty of bread and pasta (the dreaded carbs of today), but they were balanced with protein and rounded off with veggies and fruit. We were lean, fit, and enjoyed everything we ate. We were taught to be conscious of where food came from, and the importance of preparing and meal planning. The most important part of any meal was the sharing of food with family, friends, and the unexpected guests we treated just like family.

I moved out of state as a young adult, and my parents stayed behind. They were in the minority of their generation. While most of their contemporaries pined for the open space and single-family homes of the suburbs, my parents remained in my grandparents' house. How lucky I am that they stayed in Brooklyn. Eventually I returned to raise a family of my own in gentrified Park Slope, which, wasn't really Brooklyn according to my Bensonhurst-centric family!

The Bensonhurst of the 1970s and 1980s might have been an historic Italian enclave, but we did not lack opportunities to explore the food of other cultures. On any given Sunday morning before Mass, my father would make me take a run to Borough Park to bring home bagels, lox, stuffed derma, and smoked white fish from the Jewish neighborhood next-door.

In 1972, my brother, Robert, was one of a handful of neighborhood kids to travel to Brooklyn Technical High School in Fort Greene. He later became the first college graduate in our family. Following in the path of our father, he now leads the world food court for us—our family's Anthony Bourdain. Just by listening to your accent or hearing your last name, Robert can discuss your heritage, geography, and indigenous food, whether you hail from China, Bangladesh, Pakistan, Greece, Turkey, Italy, Spain, or Portugal.

Sitting on the stoop of the 1926 house we grew up in. Left to right, my grandmother, Louisa; my mother in the baby carriage; my grandmother's niece Mary; my mother's oldest sister, Madeline

I proudly graduated from the same inner-city high school as our folk hero Vinnie Barbarino, and danced beside many a Tony Manero in the hood, never realizing how the iconic "dems and dose" of Brooklyn-speak would affect my life. After graduating with honors from a prestigious art school and working as a creative director, I was made painfully aware of my parlance by a major network television executive. She recommended I enlist a speech therapist because speaking like a "kid from Brooklyn" would hinder my career. Success in graphic design did not equate with my vernacular.

The Italian American community in little-known Mapleton Park, at the northern edge of Bensonhurst, was my playground from the 1960s through the 1980s. Its provincial atmosphere was derived from an old-world sense of connection to Italy's feudal past. Each town took pride in setting itself apart from its neighbors. The same can be said for the streets, blocks, and avenues in and around Bensonhurst.

Each parish felt different. Every five-block radius seemed to have its own butcher, vegetable store, pastry shop, fish store, and salumeria. We were also supplied by the vendors wheeling pushcarts of vegetables, a daily catch of fish, seltzer, *chavel* (bleach), and ice cream wagons, of course. Our days hinged on the opening and closing of each of these wonderful shops.

Left: My son, Luca, sitting on the stoop of my mother's house; Right: an iconic silhouette of our beloved St. Rosalia church.

The house I lived in was a haven to me. Here we mourned an assassinated president and witnessed the impeachment of another. We hunkered down in the dense heat of blackouts and air raid drills. We protested the Vietnam War and, at its end, we raised a glass to peace. We used every square inch of our street as a playground. We danced to the Beatles, aspired to touch the moon. We survived the "Summer of Sam" and busing experiments for the desegregation of schools.

The Twin Towers, in the distance, just newly built, glittered in the summer haze. They seemed to hold the promise of a better tomorrow; the promise of a Manhattan which, although just across the water, felt a million miles away.

The 1960s and 1970s had a soundtrack of Sinatra songs broadcast from WNEW's *Make Believe Ballroom* with William B Williams. My grandparents spun Arturo Toscanini, Sergio Bruni, Perry Como, Jussi Björling, and Claudio Villa on their turntable. There were endless conversations about what was fresh at the market, who was cooking, what was on sale, how many people were eating, what we would cook tomorrow, and when the fish man was coming. Snippets of these conversations also became soundtracks, comfortable backgrounds spanning our lives as we did homework (or not); played punch ball, slap ball, or combat; built go-carts and scooters; told ghost stories on my cousin's stoop; shared a roller skate with a friend who didn't have one; and, of course, collected metal and paper to recycle in exchange for dollars. Rich and poor labeling was not part of our vocabulary. We all felt safely in the middle, without an abundance of anything but enough to live.

An excursion "off the block" was often a walk with grandma to Boun Gusto on 14th Avenue and 65th Street, four blocks away. Olive oil urns still stand in the basement of what is now a tile store. Back then, I watched grandma pick out vegetables and fruit. I felt at home by her side as she limped along. "*Fa male a cosh*," (my hip hurts), she would mutter, her shopping cart shimmying as we strolled. My mom took over the cart when my grandmother's age limited her walks, later transitioning to the standard-shift 1960 Rambler. Motorized shopping allowed us to travel further as our Italian specialty shops diminished. Perhaps it was why they faded.

I remember venturing southeast to 18th Avenue, passing shops such as Joe Leo Butcher and Sbarro. Mrs. Sbarro, or Mamma Sbarro, always impressed me with both her grace and class. She seemed like a film star straight out of Cinema Italia, and would have looked right at home nestled against Marcello Mastroianni's arm. After Sbarro's, we would press on to Martino's Latticini (the aroma of smoked mozzarella still brings me there to this day), Valencia, DaVinci's, Little Records, Bianco Bakery, Amato Bakery, and finally to none other than Henry's Fish Market. The vendors faces are a lasting memory.

Left to right: Our backyard clothesline; fruit and vegetable market on 69th Street; DaVinci Pizzeria on 18th Avenue, Brooklyn

Left to right: 8mm frame image of my beautiful mother en route to California; stuffed calamari that launched our journey across the United States; me in Wyoming, 1966

Our family ventured beyond the borders of Bensonhurst in 1966, taking a month-long roadtrip to visit our great-uncle Jim, who had opened a pizzeria in a suburb of Los Angeles. We celebrated the start of our adventure with a stuffed calamari dinner prepared by my Aunt Jo and Uncle Joe. We left their small 44th Street apartment after dinner and the impression stays with me still: The gift of a special meal prepared with love as a send off. There were tears as we departed towards the unknown. There were a lot of unknowns at that time, especially for a family that wouldn't allow you to go around the block, let alone on a 3,000-mile trip across the country. And certainly no one should leave hungry!

Fast forward to 1995, my second year living in the North End of Boston. I sat watching late-night television on a lonely Friday night. A talk-show host was interviewing John Travolta. After discussing Travolta's most recent movie, the host referred to a memorable scene from *Saturday Night Fever*. I was riveted as Travolta spoke about what was, to young Brooklynites, our anthem. He spoke in slow, meaningful phrases of the metaphoric scene where he gets out of his car under the Verrazzano Bridge, a place I have also been. It was a proud and inspirational moment.

Travolta's honest portrayals of Brooklyn youth holds a special place for me. I think of my own Brooklyn identity. Much of it was about how true he was to the character in the film, his struggle to find his path, to become someone. There was an awkwardness in being from a place that people labeled by virtue of our Brooklyn accent. With time that awkwardness would become a source of pride. My journey began that night, as Travolta spoke of his own horizons. It would be a search that eventually led me back to the place that played a big part in my own life: Brooklyn.

The following pages are my way of suspending time in my small corner of the world. A time of pride in a place filled with festive Italian American life, culture, and food. My Bensonhurst was the world before the media tapped into it. It will be the world should the Brooklyn hype fade. A time when environmental protection, artisanal cooking, cultural tolerance, and slow food weren't phrases but concepts our community abided by.

Me in my Huk-A-Poo shirt during my high school graduation dinner. With grandma Louisa at Silver Star Chinese Restaurant, 18th Avenue, Brooklyn, 1976.

GO-TO SHOPS

Grabbing hold of my grandmother's shopping cart years ago led me to a world of culinary delights. I still love to roam the streets of Bensonhurst, exploring the shops, old and new, and reconnecting with those special times.

I Negozi: The Shops
Page 26

Queen Ann Ravioli
Page 38

Royal Crown Il Paneantico
Page 44

Faicco's Pork Store
Page 52

Villabate Alba
Page 60

Frank & Sal
Page 68

Savarese Italian Pastry Shop
Page 76

Pastosa Ravioli
Page 84

Lioni
Page 90

Papa Pasquale
Page 96

United Meat Market
Page 100

D. Coluccio & Sons
Page 106

A.L.C. Alimentari
Italian Grocery
Page 112

Sea Breeze II
Page 116

I Negozi: The Shops

My research has given me a vivid behind-the-counter sense of some of the daily struggles these small yet precious shops experience: clients with impossible expectations; critical suppliers changing business models forcing shop owners to think fast or lose their livelihoods. Families, who years back serviced a five-block radius, now struggle with endless marketing and the constant retrofitting of their handcrafted products to an ever wider geographic area, while modern culture threatens to engulf them.

In many instances, documenting these shops meant many visits to storefronts carrying pounds of equipment with every possibility of being asked to come back another time. Proof of legitimacy and respect was paramount. It required traditional analog communication that our modern-day devices have rendered obsolete. One store owner I spoke to in a rare phone call questioned my motivation, presuming I was more interested in dating his sister than writing a book. When all else failed, however, the simple mention of my mom's name, coupled with my dedication and persistence, allowed me access I had only imagined.

Mario, master pastry chef, Savarese Italian Pastry Shop, New Utrecht Avenue, Brooklyn

The aesthetics of the colorful shops evoke the work of artist Joseph Cornell. They are scaled, reality-based, dimensional deconstructions of the green, white, and red Italian flag; an impressionistic shadowbox homage to Italian heritage.

Top: Pastosa Ravioli. Left to right: Romeo Meats; Papa Pasquale; S.A.S. Italian Records, outside and inside.

Entering each shop is equivalent to entering the owner's home. Hanging on the wall are postcards from the old country, family portraits, and signed photographs of long-gone crooners.

Sadly, as Italian Americans slowly migrate out of the neighborhood for a "better" life, the number of shops has decreased dramatically. Change has pressed me to document as much as I can before the next cherished institution locks its doors for the last time.

Through the anecdotes of the butchers, bakers, and fishmongers, each visit added to my understanding of my former neighborhood.

I heard from families of entrepreneurs. In reflecting on the care they took in the day-to-day operation of their respective crafts, you sense the uncompromising commitment to tradition. A dedication to customer satisfaction and not solely to a price point is a golden rule.

Each shop's atmosphere is colored by the commonality of ancestoral culinary history, enriched by the generations who waited in lines amidst the "oohs" and "aaaahs" inspired by aromas I now cherish. In their heart of hearts, shop owners would offer what they produce for no sum, but simply for the joy on their patrons' faces.

Tony of Frank & Sal, 18th Avenue, Brooklyn

Pride runs deep for the staff and patrons. Owners have survived many hardships. I gained a sense of what it means to live and breathe for the love of the trade and profession. Not one of them would do it any differently. One man showed me a thirty-year-old black and white photograph he carries in his backpack. It was an image of him inside the pork store he once had. His expression in the photograph was the same as he manages the counter in his current job.

Nino, Anthony, and George of Bari Pork Store, 18th Avenue, Brooklyn

Storefront of S.A.S Records, 18th Avenue, Brooklyn

There were two Italian import shops on 18th Avenue: S.A.S. Italian Records and Little Records. S.A.S. Italian Records has a particularly poignant story of defiance, passion, loss, and renewal. In addition to music, there is never a shortage of Italian fragrances, Napoli soccer shirts, espresso makers, movies, tomato sieves, and pasta machines.

Although Ciro and Rita Conte speak Neapolitan, they are from Lazio near Rome. Their father was drafted by Mussolini's military as a young man, but their grandmother refused to allow her son to fight on the side of the fascist dictator. The family packed up and took to the sea in their grandfather's fishing boat, sailing to Tunisia and remaining there until the end of World War II.

The family eventually emigrated to Brooklyn, by way of the Bronx, opening their historic Italian import shop on 18th Avenue in 1967. Since then, the Contes have worked rigorously to promote the best of Italian culture to New York City.

In the 1970s, the Contes invested all of their resources in the first professional United States soccer match against an Italian professional team—a one-time cultural exchange between team Napoli and the New York Cosmos at the new Giants Stadium in Meadowlands.

The day of the event brought torrential rain, canceling the match. The effort nearly bankrupted the family. Undeterred, the Contes continue to provide authentic Italian products to the faithful—as they have for the past 50 years.

Neighboring shop owner, Fredo, of Queen Ann Ravioli, 18th Avenue, Brooklyn

Little Records specialized in Italian music. It was named in honor of "Little Tony" Antonio Ciacci, an Italian pop singer born in 1941 in Tovoli, Italy.

Antonio Garritano, owner of Little Records, on the day it closed in 2014

Antonio Garritano opened Little Records more than 45 years ago. It was a special place for me. It was full of Italian pop culture. Most of our Italian music was purchased there: Buti, Bruni, Lanza, Villa, Pizzi, De Stefano, and Arbore. Mr. Garritano knew me as one of his many customers, at times recognizing me as the son of Anna from "the bank."

Mr. Garritano was the friend and promoter of Little Tony, who started his own record label, named Little Records. Mr. Garritano—a disk jockey in Italy during the 1950s and 1960s—adopted the name for his own record store. I spent a few hours with Mr. Garritano on his final day at Little Records as he spoke with sorrowful recognition of the end of an era. When the doors closed that evening, they would never reopen. His record shop was always filled with wonderful music, piped out to the sidewalk for the benefit of passers-by.

When I arrived on that day, the only sound was Mr. Garritano's distant Italian-English voice echoing from the back of his now dormant store. He was navigating the phone company's automated change of address for him and his ailing sister living in the apartment above.

As we looked through his memorabilia, we shared the loss and longing for a neighborhood that once was. My mom and I were linked by the emotional tie of Italian music. That connection to his shop will be sorely missed. Luckily, I got to know Mr. Garritano—*un dono della vita*, a gift of life.

Louis Coluccio, Jr., A.L.C Alimentari Italian Grocery; one of the latest examples of next-generation Italian eateries

The joy of producing this memoir was hearing the inside stories of the people and places I have known for so many years. I am thankful to see them in a new light.

These spirited places represent our collective kitchens, our shared lives and celebrations. The immigrant's mindset of carrying on is reenacted daily, honoring the truism that anything worth remembering takes the enrichment of time, sacrifice, and above all, commitment.

These shops are evocative of the kitchen table of yesteryear.
They are keepers of Italian American traditions and culture.
Brooklyn would be a poorer place if not for their owners'
passion and dedication.

Vito of J & V Pizzeria, 18th Avenue, Brooklyn

Queen Ann Ravioli

7205 18th Avenue
Brooklyn, New York, (718) 256-1061

Left to right: Frank, George, George Jr., and Fredo of Queen Ann.

Fredo sold and serviced pasta manufacturing equipment after arriving in the United States. He still repairs his 1912 Gevasco, Cavagnaro & Ambrette pasta machine himself. He pointedly explains that it folds the pasta dough with less friction, resulting in less burning and leading to a better taste.

Above: Queen Ann's famous ravioli is made on Thursdays—it's a special day.
Opposite: Fredo dusting the ravioli with corn meal, ready for packaging.

Torta di Pasta

Maccheroni pie is a great use of leftover pasta. Slice it into wedges and use sauce. Serves 6 to 8.

1 pound cooked spaghetti, al dente
8 large eggs, beaten
¼ cup whole milk
1½ teaspoons salt, plus more for cooking pasta
½ teaspoon freshly ground black pepper
¾ cup grated Romano cheese
¼ cup minced dried sausage
1 tablespoon unsalted butter
1 tablespoon olive oil

Preheat the oven to 350°F.

Bring large pot of salted water to a boil over high heat. Add the spaghetti and cook for about 8 minutes or until firm to the bite. Drain the spaghetti and set aside to cool.

Whisk the eggs, milk, salt, and pepper in a large bowl until evenly combined. Fold in the cheese, sausage, and spaghetti, tossing until the pasta is well coated.

Melt the butter and olive oil in a 10-inch ovenproof skillet on the stove over medium heat. A nonstick skillet is preferable. Add the spaghetti mixture to the skillet. Cook about 5 minutes until the bottom is golden brown. Transfer the skillet to the oven and cook for 15 to 20 minutes or until the egg is no longer runny. For additional char, broil about 3 minutes, until the top is golden brown. Cool in the skillet for 5 to 10 minutes.

Place a plate over the pan while holding the handle using oven mitts or a kitchen towel. Firmly press the plate against the pan and flip. Then flip the torta again onto the platter that you will ultimately serve it in. Cut into wedges and serve.

Royal Crown II Paneantic

6308 14th Avenue
Brooklyn, New York, (718) 234-3208

Joseph Generoso holding a photograph of his family taken in the 1960s

After arriving from Calabria, Italy, and working at his uncle's pastry shop on Bleecker Street, Joseph Generoso, his brother, Frank, and their mom, developed a bread modeled on loaves made for the fishermen's long days at sea. The Generosos's bread miraculously maintained its heartiness, freshness, and texture for days. It was "artisinal" before that phrase was uttered in the Brooklyn culinary buzz. This wonderful bread made an impression on our family from the moment the original Royal Crown Bakery opened in 1987. I remember the day my dad first brought home a loaf of Paesano bread. The expression on his face was that of a man who had just won the lottery.

Paneantico's beautiful Paesano loaf.

Formerly the Bianco Bakery oven, this original oven extends almost 20 feet into the backyard. For more than 100 years, this enormous coal oven has been and still is a hearth of joy for so many of us.

Zeppole di San Giuseppe

These are beautifully decadent pastries for the Feast of Saint Joseph, the patron saint of a happy death. Serves 10 to 12.

Batter:
1 cup water
3 tablespoons butter
½ teaspoon sugar
Pinch of salt
1 cup flour
4 eggs
1 pastry bag with star-shaped tip

Filling:
2 egg yolks
¼ cup sugar
1 tablespoon flour
1 cup milk
Peel of one lemon
1 pastry bag with star-shaped tip
Amarena Fabbri wild cherries in syrup

For the batter, pour the water into a saucepan and add the salt and butter. Bring to a boil, while stirring.

Add the flour, leaving the pan on the heat. Mix well using a spoon until the batter is smooth and no longer sticks to the sides of the pan. Remove the pan from the heat and transfer the batter to a bowl to cool. Once it reaches room temperature, add the eggs, one at a time, and mix together. When the batter is fairly light and airy, place the dough in the refrigerator for at least 20 minutes.

In the meantime, prepare the pastry filling by pouring the milk into a saucepan over medium heat. Add the lemon peel and bring to a boil, stirring continuously. Beat the egg yolks in a separate bowl, along with the sugar. Then, whisking continuously, incorporate the flour. Once the milk begins to boil, remove it from the heat and slowly add the egg, sugar, and flour mixture, whisking as you go. The resulting mixture should be soft and creamy. Transfer the mixture to the stove over medium heat. Stir continuously until the cream reaches a pudding-like texture. Once ready, pour the cream into a bowl and cover with plastic wrap and cool.

Be sure to cover the bowl well, to ensure that a film doesn't form on the surface of the cream. Prepare the fitters while you wait for the cream to cool.

Place the fritter batter (refrigerated dough) in a pastry bag with a star-shaped tip. Cut out 2-inch squares of parchment paper. Using the pastry bag, form a ring of dough on each piece of parchment until you have used all the batter. Fill a pot with frying oil and place over high heat. Once hot (325°F with a thermometer), place the fritters in the oil, two at a time. The parchment won't burn.

Do not cook more than two at a time or the oil will not stay hot. The parchment will separate from the fritters in the hot oil so you can remove it. Once brown (after 3 to 4 minutes), remove the fritters using a slotted spoon and place them to drain on paper towels while you fry the remaining batter. When the fritters are cool enough to handle, fill another pastry bag with pastry cream. Decorate each fritter with a little cream and place a cherry on top. Sprinkle with powdered sugar and enjoy the decadence.

Faicco's Pork Store

6511 11th Ave
Brooklyn, New York, (718) 236-0119

Matt and Louie holding a portrait of their grandfather, and standing in the cold room used for conditioning their dried sausage and soppressata

Matt and Louie are the third generation of a family originating in Salerno, Italy. Their grandfather opened the original 13th Avenue Faicco's shop in the 1930s.

I once told my children, if Faicco's ever closed its doors, we may have to pack up and move out of Brooklyn—a statement reflecting the uncompromising dedication at the heart of Faicco's. You experience Faicco's expertise from the moment you enter its Brooklyn store. The fragrance of smoked mozzarella fills the air in its current location on 11th Avenue between 65th and 66th streets. Faicco's was my mother's go-to for her absolute favorite hot fennel sausage.

I was enthralled in Faicco's in the way a sports fan might be about meeting their favorite athlete. I presented Matt and Louie with old photographs of the store. In one, Louie spotted an image of Berni, a beloved counterman who passed away years before. Louie, not outwardly a softie, solemnly paused, nodded, and then carried off pounds of sausage for an outgoing order. As a former student of architecture, Louie gave up the profession to help his grandfather and father—true commitment. There is great pride amongst the brotherhood behind the counter as they carry on a tradition of making the best sausage this side of the Atlantic.

Above: Matt and Louie forever supporting and supplying the countermen of Faicco's

Arancini

Faicco's rice balls are pictured, but the recipe is under lock and key. All I know is an ice cream scooper is used to make their round form. Makes 16 rice balls.

4 cups water or chicken broth
Sea salt to taste
2 cups of long grain white rice
2 tablespoons butter
1 cup whole milk ricotta cheese, drained
½ cup mozzarella cheese, shredded
1 cup grated Romano cheese
2 tablespoons chopped fresh parsley
1 teaspoon freshly ground black pepper
1 tablespoon sea salt
5 egg yolks
1½ cups breadcrumbs
1 cup flour
4 cups canola oil, for frying
Additional sea salt to taste
½ cup cured minced Italian ham, optional

Bring the water (or broth) and ¼ teaspoon salt to a boil in a medium saucepan over medium-high heat. Stir in the rice, reduce the heat to low, cover, and simmer about 20 minutes until tender. Once cooked, add the butter to the hot rice and stir until melted throughout. Spread the rice on a parchment-lined baking sheet and let cool completely.

Combine the mozzarella, Romano cheese, ricotta, salt, pepper, and chopped parsley in a bowl and set aside.

Beat two egg yolks in a large bowl, then add and stir in the cooled rice and the cheese mixture. Shape the mixture into 16 2-inch balls. If adding the minced ham, make a well in the center of each ball, insert the ham, and seal back into a ball. Refrigerate the balls for at least one hour.

Heat the oil in an 8-by-4-inch pot over medium heat (a small deep fryer works best) until it reaches 350°F on a deep-fry thermometer. Meanwhile, prepare your batter station. Place the flour and breadcrumbs in two small bowls. Whisk the remaining three eggs into a third bowl. Coat each chilled rice ball in flour, then cover in egg, and roll in bread crumbs.

Working in batches, fry the rice balls about 3½ to 4 minutes, turning them until golden brown on all sides. Remove with a slotted spoon and drain on a rack or paper towel. Season with salt to your liking. Let cool and enjoy.

Villabate Alba

7001 18th Avenue
Brooklyn, New York, (718) 331-8430

Emanuele "Manny" Alaimo opened Villabate in 1968, named after a town in Sicily. Emanuele worked at the Rex bakery and the Normandie bakery and he opened Villabate in what was formerly the Gentile bakery. In 2005, Emanuele bought the adjacent and legendary Alba Pastry. During my limited time in its kitchen, I was struck by the remarkable energy and vitality, which came in stark contrast to the changing demographic of the neighborhood.

These cannoli are every bit the sensually rich perfection they appear

The people of Sicily take pride in their ricotta. None is more delicate than that used in Villabate's cassata.

I have been intrigued by the Cezanne-inspired marzipan fruit that adorns most Italian pastry shops, ever since I was a child. I was introduced to confectionery artist Giacomino. He works in a quiet studio-like space in Villabate. Splattered with splashes of pigment, he has been performing his artistry for more than 50 years. I was honored to have met him.

Above: Confectionery artist Giacomino at work. Opposite top: Emanuele "Manny" with his daughter, two sons, and son-in-law

Villabate's very popular semolina French-style bread—available seeded or plain.

"S" Biscotti

Villabate's "S" cookies are pictured—elemental perfection with a cup of coffee. Makes 10 to 12 cookies.

2 cups all-purpose flour
2 teaspoons baking powder
½ cup sugar
2 large eggs
¼ cup softened vegetable shortening
1 teaspoon vanilla extract
1 lemon, zest only

Preheat the oven to 350°F.

Combine the flour and baking powder in a large mixing bowl.

Combine the eggs, sugar, shortening, and lemon zest in another bowl. Add the mixture to the dry ingredients and combine until all the flour has been absorbed by the egg mixture. Gather the dough into a ball and cover the bowl with plastic wrap and refrigerate for 30 minutes.

Line a cookie sheet with parchment paper.

Remove the dough from the refrigerator. Working on a lightly floured surface, break off a handful of dough at a time and roll it into an even 1-inch diameter strand. Cut the strand into small pieces, approximately 5 inches long. Place the pieces onto the prepared cookie sheet 1½ inches apart, and shape each into an "S."

Bake in the preheated oven for 20 to 30 minutes, or until edges are brown. Classico!

Frank & Sal

8008 18th Avenue
Brooklyn, New York, (718) 331-8100

Frank Gassoso came to Brooklyn in 1977 from Acri in Calabria, Italy. He began work at the well-known Trunzo Brothers Meat Market, then opened the renowned Frank & Sal in 1986. Its hallmark is aged beef, plus daily lunch and dinner specials. It's the perfect combination of a tavola calda and a fully stocked salumeria.

Today his son Frank, Jr. carries on managing the traditions and typical flavors of their hometown province. Their shop has the essence and authenticity of old-world Italy, evidenced by many Italian-speaking customers. On certain days, you can find fresh rabbit, capuzzelle, tripe, cotene (pig skin), and even succulent pork liver.

Frank Gassaso prides himself on old-world butchery and care in aging prime meat

Salsa di Pomodoro Cruda

Both my parents would make this sauce in the summer. My mom, because it did not require much tending, and my dad, because it was simple enough for him to make. It reminds me of our cherished summer vacations on Cape Cod. Serves 6 to 8.

2 pounds ripe cherries cut in half
4 cloves cracked garlic
6 tablespoons extra virgin olive oil
6 branches of fresh basil, leaves only
1 tablespoons salt and black pepper, or to taste
4- to 6-quart pot
1 pound dry pasta, preferably spaghetti
½ teaspoon grated pecorino Romano cheese for topping, optional
A warm and sunny summer day

Slice the cherry tomatoes using a sharp knife and add them to a 4- to 6-quart pot.

Separate the leaves from three of the six basil sprigs. Fold in salt, extra virgin olive oil, and the basil leaves using a large wooden spoon.

If you are away from home, cover the tomatoes with a glass lid. If the pot has no lid, use cling film wrap to cover the top of the pot. Place the pot in direct sunlight for several hours. I have left it to ripen for up to five hours. You can also speed up the process with the traditional method of heating it on the stove until tomatoes become soft.

The salt and heat will break down the tomatoes and produce delicious juicy goodness. This is the time to dip in a crusty piece of bread to taste.

Slice the rest of the basil and add more if you prefer. Bring a large pot of water to a boil. Add salt, then pasta, and bring back to boil. Cook until the pasta is al dente. Strain the pasta, reserving a cup of pasta water. Place the pasta back in the pot, fold in some of the fresh tomatoes, torn or sliced basil, and juice. Add some of the pasta water if needed.

Top with additional fresh tomato sauce when serving, a dash of extra virgin olive oil, and either Romano or Parmigiana grated cheese. This sauce represents summer vacation at its best.

Savarese Italian Pastry Shop

5922 New Utrecht Avenue
Brooklyn, New York, (718) 438-7770

In 1955, Mario's older brother Anthony arrived in America from Venosa, in the Basilicata region. While Mario was serving with the United States Army in Korea, Anthony became the apprentice baker for the legendary Salvatore Alba at Cammareri's on 86th Street. In 1961, Anthony and Mario bought Savarese Italian Pastry Shop. The brothers worked side by side until 1995. Today Mario carries on the family tradition in fine baking, working alongside his two sons, Joseph and Pasquale.

The always jovial Mario often quotes the Roman philosopher Quinto Orazio Flacco, also from Venosa. He fondly refers to bakers who have worked at his shop. I once greeted Mario as the "il padre" of the local bakers, based on the many who have either worked or apprenticed at Savarese. He modestly deflected my compliment.

Above: The original corner location of Savarese. The shop was originally owned by the Starace family from Sorrento, Italy, relations on my grandmother's side of the family.
Below: Savarese's Italian ice is creamy goodness, always in a paper cup.

No trip to Savarese's is complete without a taste of its famous Italian ice. It's the same icy richness I have savored since I was able to reach the counter. There isn't a summer I don't recall walking home, to the rhythms of the elevated train, savoring the sweet Brooklyn nights, with an Italian ice in hand. The magic lies in its perfect balance of flavor and silkiness, fashioned from an age-old artisanal use of ice and salt. The chocolate ice is the best in Brooklyn, if not the nation. One Memorial Day, when we had our first cups of ice after a long winter, my daughter exclaimed, "Daddy, I forgot how good this was!"

Facing page top: The original corner location of Savarese The shop was originally owned by the Starace family from Sorrento, Italy, relations on my grandmother's side of the family

Facing page below:
Savarese's Italian ice, creamy goodness, always in a paper cup.

Taralli al Limone

These cookies bring together the sourness of the lemon, richness of the butter, and sweetness of the frosting into an alchemical wonder.

Batter:
3 eggs
¾ cup butter, softened
1 teaspoon vanilla extract
1 cup sugar
3 cups all-purpose flour
1 tablespoon baking powder
Dash of salt
1 tablespoon lemon juice
1 teaspoon lemon zest

Frosting:
5 egg whites
½ tablespoons lemon juice
½ tablespoons lemon zest
3 cups powdered sugar
Colored confetti for decorating, for the holidays

Preheat the oven to 375°F.

Beat the butter and sugar in the bowl of a stand mixer, until incorporated. With mixer on low to medium speed, add the eggs, vanilla, lemon juice, and lemon zest. Sift together the flour, baking powder, and salt in a separate bowl.

Fold the flour mixture into the wet ingredients. Mix the ingredients into a dough ball and refrigerate for 30 minutes. Roll into slightly flattened balls using a mounded tablespoon of dough.

Bake for 15 to 20 minutes, or until edges are just golden brown.

Mix all the frosting ingredients with a whisk until silky. Glaze the cookies when still warm, sprinkle some rainbow-colored nonpareil, and let dry before serving. These cookies were traditionaly served for the Christmas season. I always think of my cousin's grandmother Mrs. Simone every time I make them.

Pastosa Ravoli

7425 Utrecht Avenue
Brooklyn, New York, (718) 236-9615

Joseph Ajello manages his grandfather's business

Mr. Anthony Ajello, a son of Naples, Italy, became a salesman for Polly-O Italian cheese. Upon settling in Bensonhurst 50 years ago, he opened his first store. Three generations later, his grandson Joseph Ajello has become the face and pace of the Pastosa brand, offering expanded Italian fare that includes tomatoes, olive oil, and prepared food. Despite the more expansive interstate and internet reach, the shop on New Utrecht Avenue maintains a corner store feel, especially during the holiday season.

Nestled on the corner of New Utrecht Avenue and Bay Ridge Parkway, the flagship Pastosa Ravioli is filled with patrons from near and far, and standing shoulder to shoulder on the bustling days leading up to the holidays.

Sugo del Contadino

Rustic pasta dish prepared by a farmer. We always waited for the extra-ripe red and yellow tomatoes for more color. Serves 4 to 6.

1 pound spaghetti
1½ pounds cherry tomatoes, cut in half if too big
2 tablespoons fresh parsley
1¼ teaspoon fresh oregano, can use dried
6-8 tablespoon extra virgin olive oil
3 cloves garlic, sliced
18-24 green pitted olives
18-24 black or kalamata pitted olives
1 tablespoon salted capers, rinsed of excess salt
Crushed black pepper and salt to taste

Heat 2 tablespoons of the oil and sliced garlic in a 2-quart pot over medium heat. Sauté until the garlic just begins to turn golden brown. Add the oregano and allow a minute for the oregano to merge with the oil. Add the capers and black and green olives, and sauté for 2 minutes to merge the flavor with the hot oil.

Add half the fresh parsley and cook for another minute followed by all the tomatoes. Bring to a low boil, then lower the heat to a simmer and cover pan. Cook the tomatoes approximately 1 hour, until completely wilted and soft. I sometimes puncture the bigger tomatoes with a fork.

Bring a large pot of water to a boil. Add salt, then the pasta, and bring back to boil. Cook until the pasta is al dente. Strain the pasta and save a cup of pasta water. Place the pasta back in the pot, fold in some of the sauce, torn parsley, and some of the pasta water if needed.

Top with additional sauce, a dash of extra virgin olive oil, and either grated Romano or parmigiano cheese when serving.

God bless our farmers!

Lioni Latticini

7819 15th Avenue
Brooklyn, New York, (718) 232-7852

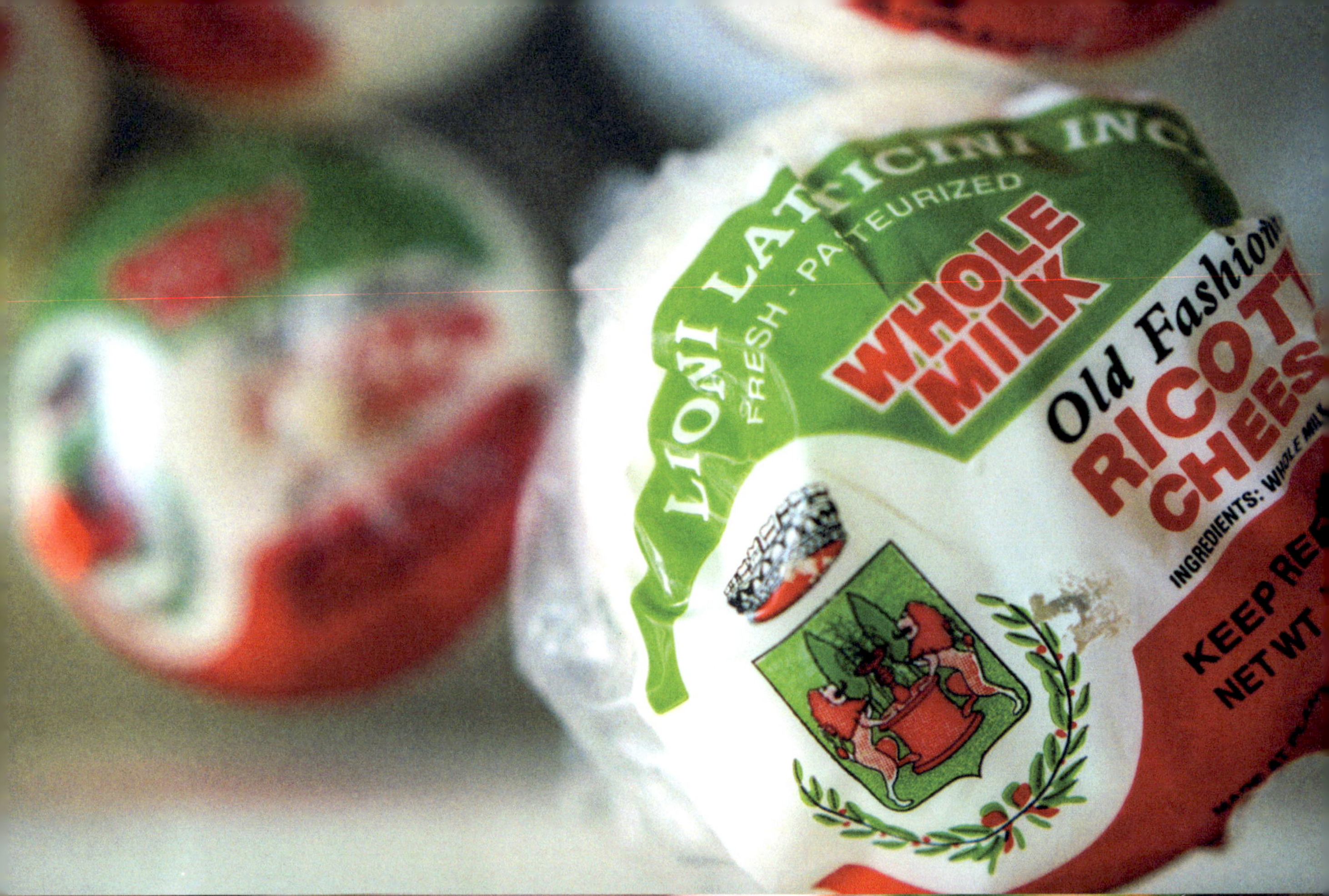
LIONI LATTICINI INC
FRESH - PASTEURIZED
WHOLE MILK

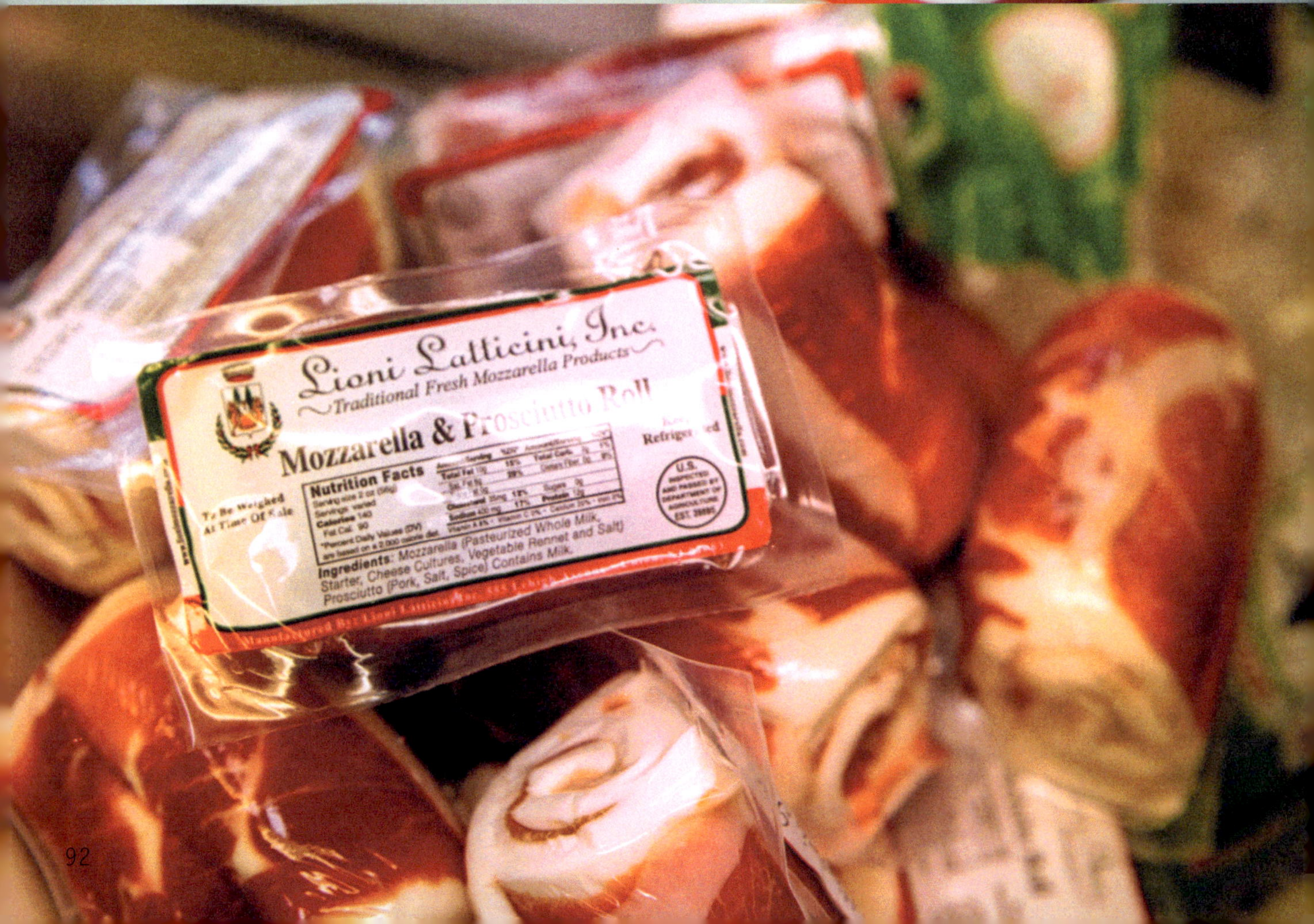
Lioni Latticini, Inc.
Traditional Fresh Mozzarella Products
Mozzarella & Prosciutto Roll
Nutrition Facts
To Be Weighed At Time Of Sale
Ingredients: Mozzarella (Pasteurized Whole Milk, Starter, Cheese Cultures, Vegetable Rennet and Salt) Prosciutto (Pork, Salt, Spice) Contains Milk.

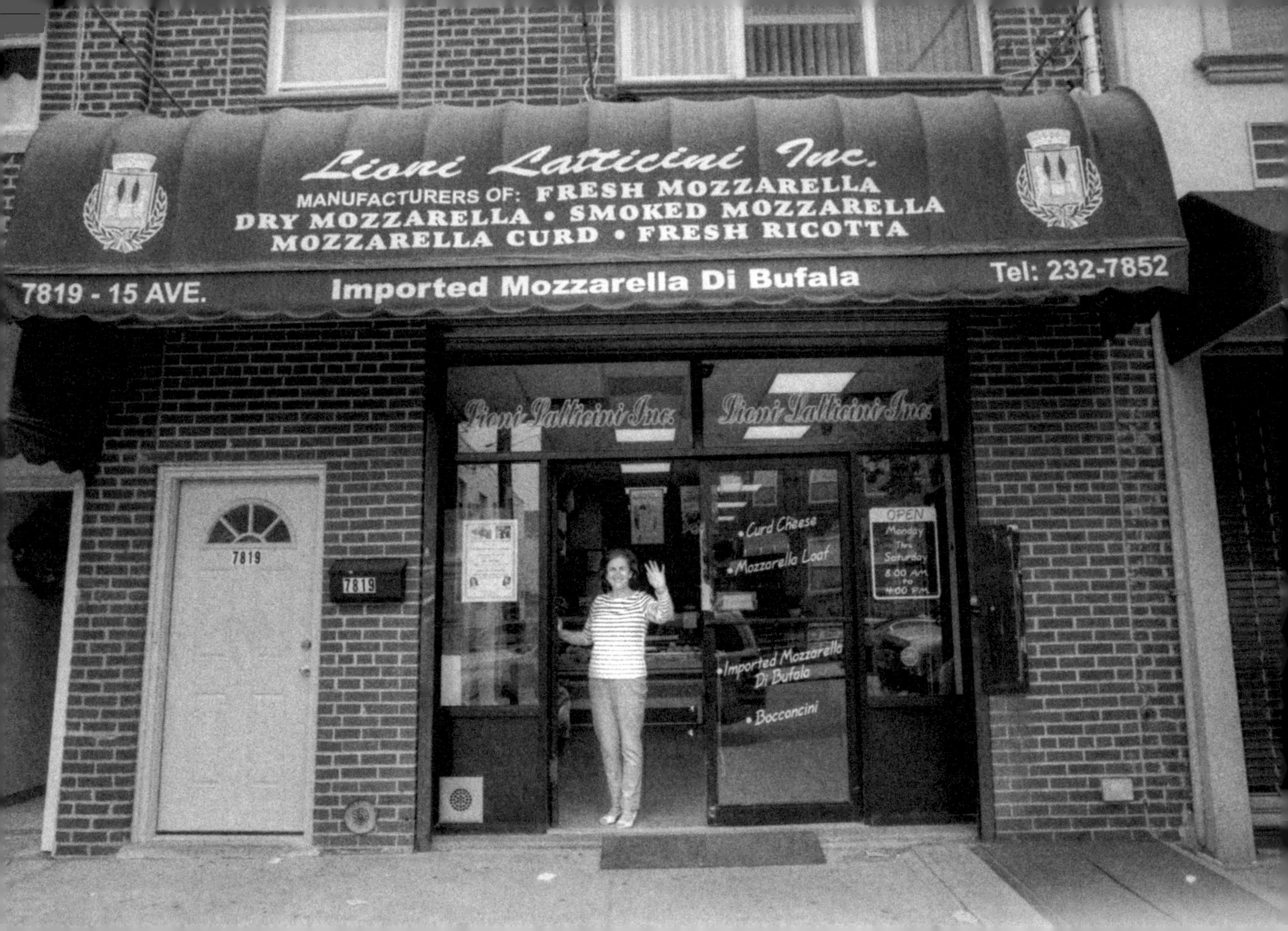
Lioni Latticini Inc.
MANUFACTURERS OF: FRESH MOZZARELLA
DRY MOZZARELLA • SMOKED MOZZARELLA
MOZZARELLA CURD • FRESH RICOTTA
7819 - 15 AVE.
Imported Mozzarella Di Bufala
Tel: 232-7852
Lioni Latticini Inc.
Lioni Latticini Inc.
7819
7819
• Curd Cheese
• Mozzarella Loaf
• Imported Mozzarella Di Bufala
• Bocconcini
OPEN
Monday
Thru
Saturday
8:00 AM
to
4:00 P.M.

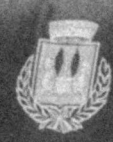

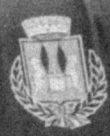

Pasta del Fornaio

A traditional pasta dish topped with pan-roasted breadcrumbs, hence "pasta of the baker." Serves 4.

1 pound fresh ricotta cheese
1½ cup dry bread crumbs
½ cup extra virgin olive oil, divided
1 cup grated pecorino Romano or parmigiano cheese
2 teaspoons fresh ground pepper
Sea salt to taste
1 pound dry pasta, preferably spaghetti
1 tablespoon chopped fresh parsley

Bring a large pot of water to the boil for the pasta. Remove the ricotta from the refrigerator, mix to loosen and set aside to reach room temperature.

Combine the bread crumbs and all but 1 tablespoon of the oil in a small bowl. Place a small skillet (preferably cast iron) over medium heat. When the pan is hot, add the bread crumbs and cook about 15 minutes, stirring, until they are lightly browned.

Place the toasted bread crumbs into a medium bowl. Add the grated cheese and half the black pepper. Stir to combine and set aside.

When the water comes to a rolling boil, add salt and the pasta. Cook about 8 to 9 minutes until the pasta is al dente. Remove, and set aside 2 cups of the cooking water before draining the pasta.

Return the pasta to the pot, add the remaining one tablespoon of olive oil, parsley, the remaining black pepper, and ricotta. Mix together while adding ladles of pasta water until the mixture is creamy.

Place the pasta mixture in a bowl, top liberally with the flavored bread crumbs, and serve.

Simple joys are always the best.

Salsiccie al Forno

Roasted sausage, potatoes, and peppers is a meal in one dish. Serves 6.

4 tablespoons olive oil
2 pounds cheese-and-parsley sausage
4 green peppers, sliced
5 medium-large Yukon Gold potatoes, halved and quartered
2-3 large sweet onions, sliced
1 large red onion, sliced
1 tablespoon dry oregano
1 pint of cherry tomatoes
2 cloves garlic, cracked
1 cup white wine
Salt and pepper to taste

Preheat the oven on to 350°F.

Cut the sausage into 4-inch pieces.

In a 12-by-18-inch ovenproof pan add olive oil, white wine, sausage, peppers, onions, potatoes, garlic, oregano, and tomatoes. Fold to coat all the ingredients with olive oil.

Roast for at least 1½ hours, stirring ingredients every so often to evenly brown.

Serve with crusty bread. It's that simple and delicious.

Papa Pasquale

7817 15th Avenue
Brooklyn, New York, (718) 232-1798

Brooklyn's Little Italy

Welcome to
PAPÁ PASQUALE'

HOME OF THE FAMOUS "5" CHEESE RAVIOLI

LEGENDARY BROOKLYN HERO'S

OLD-TIME SALUMERIA

PAPÁ

Above: Pasquale holds fond memories of where it all began. His shop is a wonderful hybrid museum of Italian American pop culture and Italian delicacies.

Pasquale is a second-generation Sicilian, whose family originated in Caltanissetta. Forty years ago, he was a delivery boy for Manzella Grocery, a neighborhood shop since 1935. In 1995, Pasquale bought Manzella's and renamed it Papa Pasquale. His shop is peppered with Italian American nostalgia. His pride is clearly represented by the vintage photographs, nostalgic food packaging, and his award-winning ravioli. Upon being asked for the recipe for his beautiful frittata with potatoes, peppers, and zucchini, he modestly said, "It's nothing of course, people are looking for nutritious simplicity." People are also looking for soul and connection. I hope Pasquale knows as well as I that he provides both.

Pepperoni Arrostiti e Pomodori Secchi

Roasted peppers and sun-dried tomato inspired by my pal Tom Nielsen while I was living in Boston's North End. Serves 4.

- 1 pound pasta, dry or fresh
- 3 tablespoons olive oil
- 1 sweet onion, minced
- 1 cup pine nuts
- 1 tablespoon large capers packed in salt, chopped
- 4-5 sweet red peppers, peeled and minced after roasting
- 2 cups sun-dried tomatoes, minced
- 1 teaspoon freshly ground black pepper
- 3 cups of marinara sauce (page 167)

Place the peppers in an ovenproof pan under the broiler. Rotate the peppers often to char on all sides. Place the peppers into a paper bag and seal or in a covered pot until they cool. Once cool enough to handle, peel away the charred skin as best you can, core out the seeds and stems, and discard.

Pour the oil into a medium-large deep skillet over medium heat. Add the onions and sauté about 10 minutes until tender and golden brown.

In the same pan, add the rinsed capers and pine nuts, and sauté for 1 minute. Stir until the pine nuts are just about a light golden color. Add the sun-dried tomatoes, marinara sauce, and roasted peppers. Mix together in the pan and simmer for 30 minutes.

Bring a large pot of water to boil. Add salt then pasta, and bring back to boil. Cook the pasta until it is al dente. Strain the pasta, and save a cup of pasta water. Place the pasta back in the pot, fold in some of the sauce, torn basil, and some of the pasta water if needed.

Top with additional sauce, a dash of extra virgin olive oil, and either grated Romano or parmigiano cheese when serving.

Thank you, Tom!

United Meat Market

219 Prospect Park West
Brooklyn, New York, (718) 768-7227

Brothers Rocco and Joe, first-generation sons of Calabria, Italy, grew up making sausage and butchering meat as part of their family routine. They were raised in a rural setting by a family that grew all the food they consumed. "Back home," salt, sugar, and dried pasta were the only products purchased at markets. Their no-waste philosophy is reflected in their efficiently run shop.

Rocco can't keep up with customer demand for their sauces

Part of my personal journey began when I was living in Boston's North End. I had settled in a predominantly Italian neighborhood that was also home to the Purity Cheese store. Here, an Italian American named Nunzio handcrafted beautiful, pillow-soft mozzarelle.

Walking into Purity Cheese evoked childhood memories of the days my mother and I visited Martino's on 18th Avenue in Brooklyn. I became interested in learning how to make mozzarella and soon after began meeting Nunzio every Saturday morning at 6:00 a.m. to assist him. I will always remember Nunzio's red hands, scalded raw by the boiling hot water in which he would knead this wonderful cheese.

When I returned to Brooklyn from Boston, I settled in southern Park Slope, down the street from United Meat Market. My family questioned whether gentrified Park Slope could be considered part of Brooklyn at all—there were too many hipsters who hadn't graduated from the "school of hard knocks." Walking into United, I felt an immediate connection to Rocco and Joe. I soon realized that, as boys in the 1970s, they had delivered provisions to my mother's doorstep from the legendary Joe Leo's Meat Market on 17th Avenue—a blast from my Bensonhurst past.

Parmigiana di Melanzane

Eggplant parmesan inspires so many interpretations—this is ours. Serves 8 to 10.

3 medium eggplants, sliced ½-inch thick.
Coarse sea salt
1 cup all-purpose flour
3 large eggs
2 cups bread crumbs
1 cup canola oil
½ cup extra virgin olive oil
2 quarts tomato sauce (page 167)
2 cups grated Parmigiana
1 pound mozzarella sliced
2 handfuls fresh basil, torn
Freshly ground black pepper to taste

Preheat the oven to 375°F.

Layer the eggplant slices in a large colander, sprinkling each layer with salt. Set aside over a rimmed plate or bowl. Remove the eggplant from the colander after 1 hour and pat dry.

Prepare three separate shallow platters—one with the flour, another with the eggs whisked with 1 teaspoon of salt, and the last with the bread crumbs. Dip each eggplant slice in that order, from left to right. First into the flour, coating both sides, then into the egg to coat well, and lastly into the bread crumbs. Make sure all sides are coated with each ingredient. Place the breaded slices on a cookie sheet lined with parchment paper or wire rack until ready to fry.

Heat the canola and olive oil together in a medium-heavy skillet (preferably cast iron), over medium-high heat. When the oil reaches 350°F degrees on a deep-fry thermometer, add a few slices of eggplant at a time to the oil, careful not to crowd the pan. Cook about 2 minutes until both sides are golden brown. Remove the slices from the oil and drain on paper towels. Continue to fry all of the eggplant, waiting 1 minute between batches to ensure the oil returns to temperature.

Place the tomato sauce in a 3- to 4-quart saucepan over low heat to warm slightly. Coat the bottom of a 9-by-13-by-2-inch baking dish or pan with warm tomato sauce. Add a layer of fried eggplant to cover the bottom of the pan, making sure the slices are touching and fit snugly, and using various sizes to minimize any gaps. Sprinkle grated cheese evenly over the eggplant, then add a layer of the sliced cheese.

Spread about a cup of sauce over the cheese, then add a sprinkling of the fresh basil and some freshly ground black pepper. Add the next layer in the same fashion, beginning with the eggplant, then cheeses, sauce, and seasoning, and gently press down on the layer. Repeat this process until you have used all eggplant and topping off sauce. Reserve extra cheese to top off.

After completing all of the layers, add more sauce to the spaces between slices of eggplant and around the perimeter of the pan. (This compensates for the bread crumbs absorbing much of the sauce.) Place in the preheated oven, loosely covered with aluminum foil, tenting it so it doesn't make contact with the sauce. Bake for 30 minutes, then remove the foil tent. Continue baking for another 15 minutes, until the top is gently browned. Allow baked eggplant to rest for a good 20 minutes. Cut into squares and serve in a shallow bowl.

D. Coluccio & Sons

1214 60th Street
Brooklyn, New York, (718) 436-6700

When Louie and Dominic Coluccio's father came to America, he brought his daughter, Cathy, and one single olive from Calabria, Italy. It was a symbol of their own imported brand of olive oils to come.

Coluccio's has been the go-to for all imported Italian products since 1964. Everyone, from internationally established chefs to fiercely proud homemakers, view Coluccio's as an entrypoint to the authentic food products of Italy. Louie always remembers his customers, and our whole family feels at home every time we walk into his store. It doesn't hurt that we are also happily breathing in the fragrance of Brooklyn's largest selection of imported Italian cheese.

Salsiccia e Peperoni

I also add fennel and some sauce to my sausage and peppers. Serves 8.

2 pounds fennel sausage
2 cloves garlic, coarsely chopped
2 large sweet onions, sliced
3 to 4 cups marinara sauce (page 167)
6 red bell peppers, sliced
1 small fennel bulb, sliced
1 tablespoon dried anise seeds, crushed
1 tablespoon salt
1 teaspoon freshly ground black pepper

Preheat the oven to 350°F.

Quickly brown the sausage in an ovenproof pot or Dutch oven over medium-high heat, being careful not to totally cook through. Remove from the pot and set aside.

Reduce the heat to medium-low and sauté the garlic in the same pot for 1 to 2 minutes, until it just begins to look golden. Add the onions and sauté them with the garlic, stirring frequently. When the onions are translucent, add the marinara sauce, stirring around the bottom of the pot to merge the sauce with the browning flavors of the sausage.

Remove the pot from the stove top. Cut the warm sausage into 1-inch-thick pieces, or slice lengthwise about ½-inch thick. Return the sausage to the pot, along with the peppers, fennel, anise seeds, salt, and pepper.

Gently fold all of the ingredients in the pot. Cover and place in the center of the preheated oven. Cook for 30 to 40 minutes, until the sausage is cooked and the peppers are barely soft.

Remove the pot from the oven, and serve immediately. Be mindful that the mixture will continue to cook another 5 to 10 minutes off the heat, so be careful the peppers don't get overcooked. Serve as a panino on crusty bread or in a bowl with a side of bread. Classic goodness!

Pomodori Ripieni

The first time I ate a stuffed tomato was in Rome and I never forgot it. Depending on size, this recipe stuffs 4 to 6 tomatoes. Serves 4.

2 tablespoons olive oil
2 medium white potatoes, peeled and cubed
½ cup dictvvved sweet onion
½ cup white wine
1 cup arborio or white rice
1 cup chicken or vegetable stock
½ cup grated Parmigiana cheese
1 teaspoon sea salt
1 tablespoon dried oregano
1 tablespoon fresh parsley, chopped
1 teaspoon freshly ground black pepper
4 large ripe tomatoes
2 cups marinara sauce (page 167)

Preheat the oven to 400°F. Position an oven rack in the upper third.

Heat the oil in a medium-large deep skillet over medium heat. Add the potatoes and sauté about 10 minutes, until tender and golden brown. Remove the potatoes from the pan and set aside.

Add the onion in the same pan, and sauté until translucent. Add the wine and simmer for 3 minutes or until the alcohol has cooked off. Stir in the rice and stock, cover and cook about 10 minutes until al dente.

Fold the potatoes into the rice, along with the grated cheese, salt, oregano, parsley, and pepper. Set the pan aside.

Cut the tomatoes across the top and carefully remove the core and pulp without breaking the outside walls. Add a pinch of salt to each tomato, making sure to spread it around the inside. Carefully fill each tomato to the brim with the rice mixture, and top off with 2 tablespoons. of marinara sauce. Place the stuffed tomatoes in an ovenproof dish or pan.

Add 1 inch of water to the bottom of the pan. Place the tomatoes on the upper rack of the preheated oven. Bake uncovered for approximately 30 minutes or until the tomatoes become soft.

A.L.C. Alimentari Italian Grocery

8613 3rd Avenue
Brooklyn, New York, (718) 836-6700

A second-generation son of Calabria, Italy, Louis Coluccio, Jr. learned his family's way of life the way so many of us did—by his grandparents' side. Louis knew one day he would have a shop of his own and in 2012 he opened A.L.C Alimentari Italian Grocery. Louis' shop and eatery is equally a comfort and a revelation. Alimentari refreshes Italian American culture for the next generation, while maintaining strong roots with its authentic, can't-miss recipes.

Melanzane Ripiene al Forno

Stuffed egglant is so "grandma" to me. There were many days I brown bagged a few stuffed eggplants between two pieces of bread. Serves 8 to 10.

5 small eggplants
1 cup pine nuts
1 cup extra virgin olive oil
3 cloves garlic, finely chopped
3 cups of bakery bread crumbs
½ cup grated Parmigiana cheese
2 tablespoons large capers, chopped
1 teaspoon freshly ground black pepper
3 cups of marinara sauce (page 167)

Cut the eggplants in half lengthwise. Scoop out and chop the inside pulp, leaving enough pulp within the shells to retain their firmness. (There should be approximately 3 to 4 cups of chopped eggplant.) Lightly salt the inside of the eggplant shells and let them drain.

Place the pine nuts in a medium skillet over low heat and lightly toast them, being careful they don't burn. Remove the pine nuts from the pan and set aside.

Preheat the oven to 375°F.

Heat ½ cup of the olive oil in the same pan. Add the garlic and sauté for 1 minute, then add the chopped eggplant. Continue to sauté until the eggplant is soft.

Raise the heat to medium and add the breadcrumbs to the skillet of eggplant and garlic. Brown the bread crumbs, being careful not to burn them by stirring every moment until they aregolden brown. Remove from the heat.

Add chopped capers and black pepper to the breadcrumb eggplant mixture. Mix thoroughly.

Pat the eggplant shells dry.

Fill the cavity of the eggplant half with the bread crumb mixture, pressing it down slightly into the shell. Add some tomato sauce to cover the top and decoratively add some of the remaining pine nuts. Repeat for all.

Place in a 9-by-13-by-2-inch baking inch-baking dish, and loosely tent with aluminum foil. Bake for 45 minutes and serve warm.

8500 18th Avenue
Brooklyn, New York
Closed in September 2017.

Angelo started fishing with his father in Sciacca, Sicily, at the age of 13. He entered the United States in the 1970s, and worked for the renowned Henry's Fish Market. He then partnered at Sea Breeze on 9th Avenue in Manhattan, later opening Sea Breeze II on 18th Avenue in Brooklyn, and running it for 27 years. Angelo and his wife Lillian first met when they were 10 years old. They and their children all teamed up during the busy Christmas holiday. Sea Breeze II closed in September 2017, but for me it will always represent one of the most memorable experiences of the Christmas season.

Above: Lillian. Below: friendly countermen and the always animated Angelo. Shopping for the Feast of the Seven Fishes on Christmas Eve will remain an indelible memory.

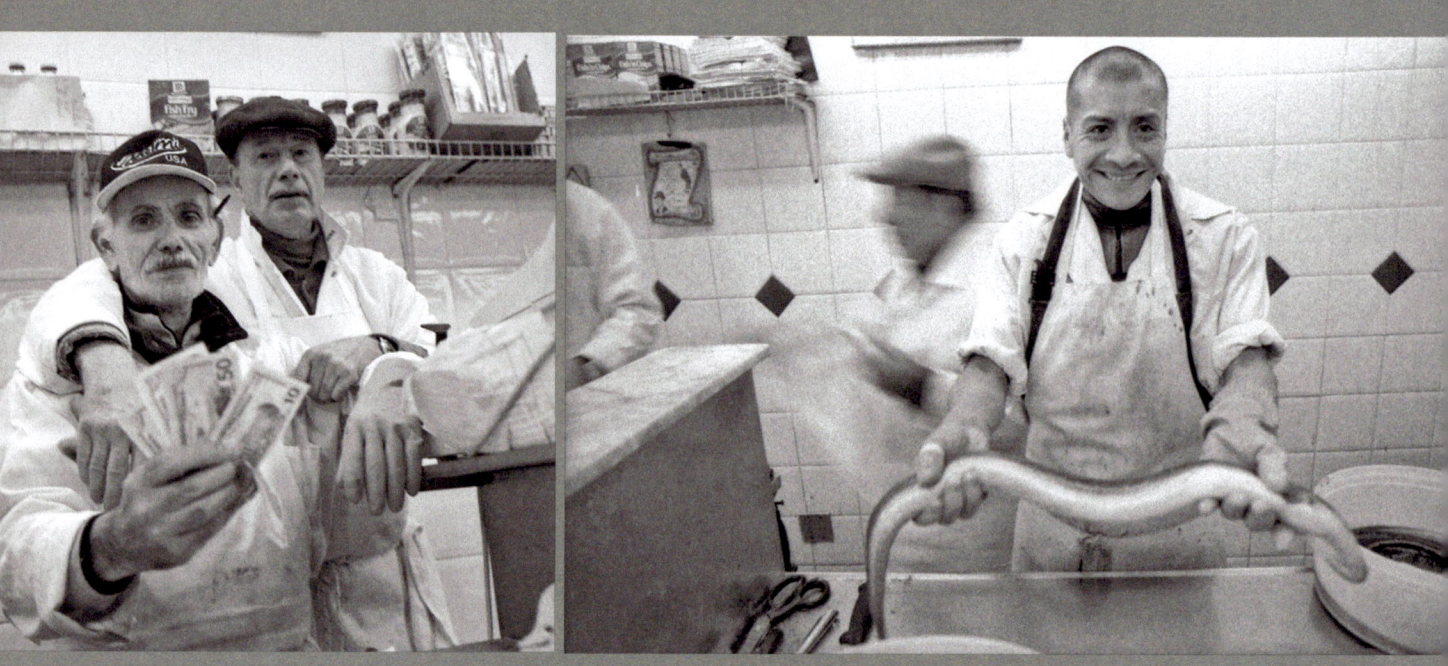

Angelo's son Joseph worked by his father's side at Sea Breeze II just as Angelo fished with his own father in Sicily

Gamberi Fra Diavolo
Shrimp with chili. Serves 4.

1 pound dry spaghetti
3 tablespoons extra virgin olive oil
1½ pounds large shrimp, peeled and deveined
3 cloves garlic, minced
Pinch of crushed red chili pepper flakes
1 teaspoon dried oregano
16 ounces marinara sauce (page 167) or plum tomatoes
    blended with juice for 5 seconds
1 teaspoon sea salt
Chopped parsley

Bring 4 quarts of water to a boil in a 6-quart pot. Add some salt and the spaghetti and cook about 8 minutes until al dente. Save at least 16 ounces of pasta water to slowly add back to the final mixture.

In the meantime, heat the olive oil in a large skillet over medium heat. Add the shrimp and sear on both sides. Remove them from the pan and set aside.

Place the minced garlic in the same skillet and sauté about 2 minutes until just golden brown. Add the red pepper flakes, tomato sauce, oregano, and salt. Bring everything to a quick simmer. Return the seared shrimp to the skillet, simmer for 1 more minute and turn off the heat. Add the cooked pasta to the sauce, toss well, add parsley and pasta water for a creamier sauce, and serve with shrimp on top.

LA FESTA

Christmas Eve, the Feast of the Seven Fishes
Page 124

Christmas Day
Page 158

Easter
Page 194

Good Friday
Page 198

Easter Sunday
Page 210

Daily Dishes
Page 224

Christmas Eve

In most Italian American homes, Vigilia di Natale (Christmas Eve) is the most solemn celebration of the year. Families wait for the midnight birth of the infant Jesus by sitting down at an elaborate meal. Seven different dishes are traditionally prepared, representing the seven sacraments or the seven days of creation. Some families, like mine, have been known to prepare 11 or even 13 dishes.

The Feast of the Seven Fishes

Stoccafisso (or *stocco*) and baccalà (dried and salted codfish). Stoccafisso is codfish that has been air dried in frigid arctic air. There was a time when these basic food staples, which could be easily stored in any dry place in your house or ship cargo, were the least expensive fish you could buy. The fish would be brought into our house two weeks before Christmas, and preparations would begin.

Sea salad
Octopus sauce
Stocco
Fried fish
Baccala salad
Stuffed escarole
Baked shrimp
Marinated eel
Scungilli
Sweet pie

To us children, the elaborate process of turning petrified fish into tender, white flesh seemed nothing short of miraculous. My mother and grandmother would always use the same porcelain-coated pan to rehydrate the fish. The faucet would be turned on to a mere trickle to rinse the salt away from the baccalà and to soften the stoccafisso.

The slow, incessant drip of the fountain would become unbearable—a form of water torture, inspiring my father's inventiveness. He realized that by tying one end of a string to the faucet and placing the other end in the bowl, he could guide the drops of tap water along the the curve of the string. This primitive form of hydrotherapy would go on for two solid weeks, the fish releasing a rich odor as it softened. The pungent smell filled the kitchen and shocked my budding olfactory senses, but the more senior members of the family seemed unaffected. They knew this suffering would lead to pure, nirvanic deliciousness.

My father's hydrating mechanism, as sketched by my brother, Robert.

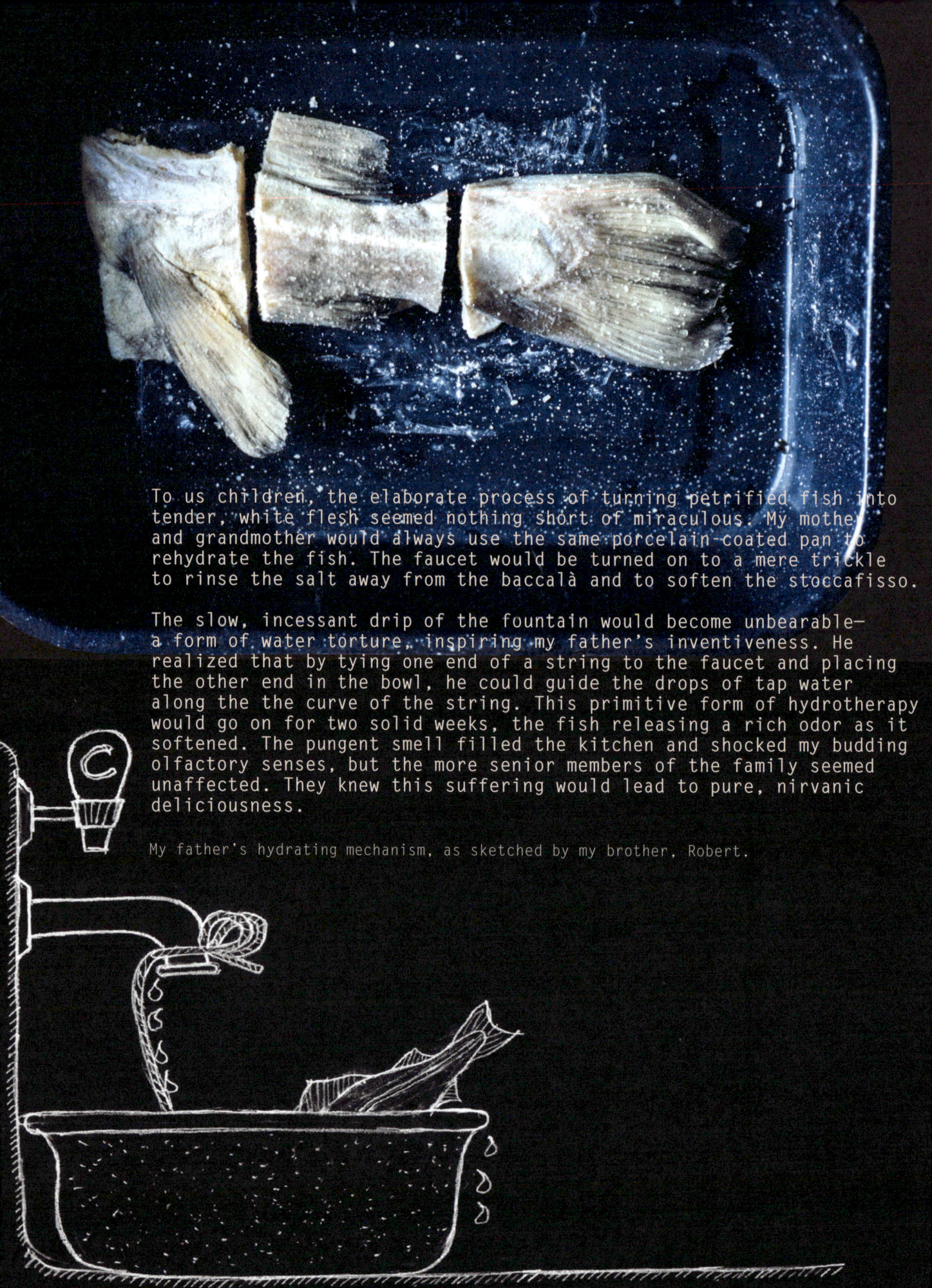

Left to right: Our favorite vintage Paramount illuminated snowman; my mother and father at our house on 61st Street; children decorating my parents' tree. Bottom: My son with his favorite electric trains—Lionels, of course.

The preparation of the stocco also served as a kind of advent calendar. The time it took to process the codfish represented the amount of time until December 24. Over the years, that olfactory overload became associated with the luminous arrival of Christmas, electric trains, joyous music, and the communal joy of preparing a feast.

The tracks to my electric trains could not be laid until all of our house (the cleanest house on our block) received additional "holiday cleaning." As the youngest, I had to assume the house-cleaning responsibilities that would (back in that day) have been assigned to a daughter. I helped polish floors, wash windows, and pleat and hang curtains in both my mother's and grandmother's apartments. I endured the humiliating domestic labor in anticipation of the moment when the housework complete, I could finally fire off my wonderful, electrified Lionel trains.

Our vintage illuminated angel

Day after day, drop after drop, water continued to stream from my grandmother's kitchen faucet. As the stocco metamorphosed, so too would our apartment. Heavyweight curtains were raised, keeping out the cold drafts that crept through age-old window panes. The low angle of the solstice sun created rainbows that refracted through the crystals of my mother's dresser and onto the gleaming linoleum floor that was freshly waxed every Saturday afternoon.

Beautifully packaged and yellowed corrugated boxes were paraded out of the garage and pulled from overhead closets. Each filled with ornamental history. In a matter of hours, the house was ablaze with our own *Albero di Natale*. This signaled the next big event, rivaled only by the birth of the Savior himself—writing the Christmas Eve menu.

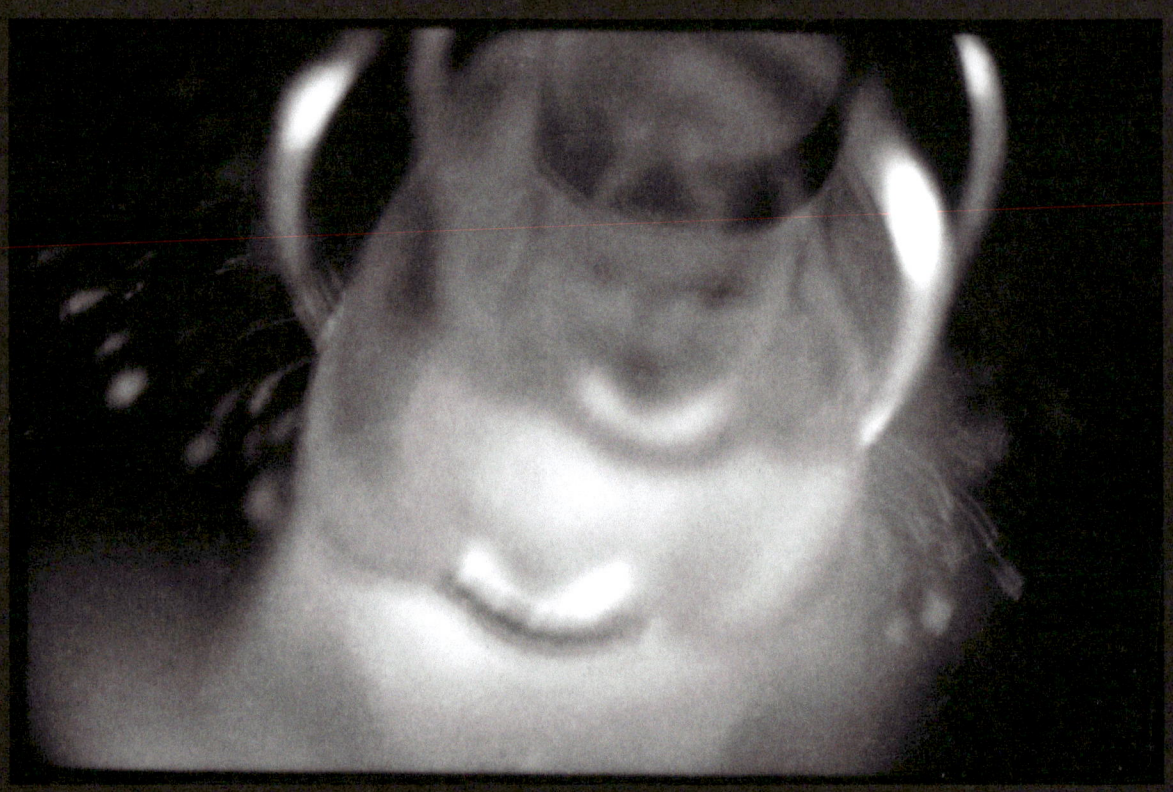

Floured fish for the fritto misto, and my son, Luca, staring down the traditional eel

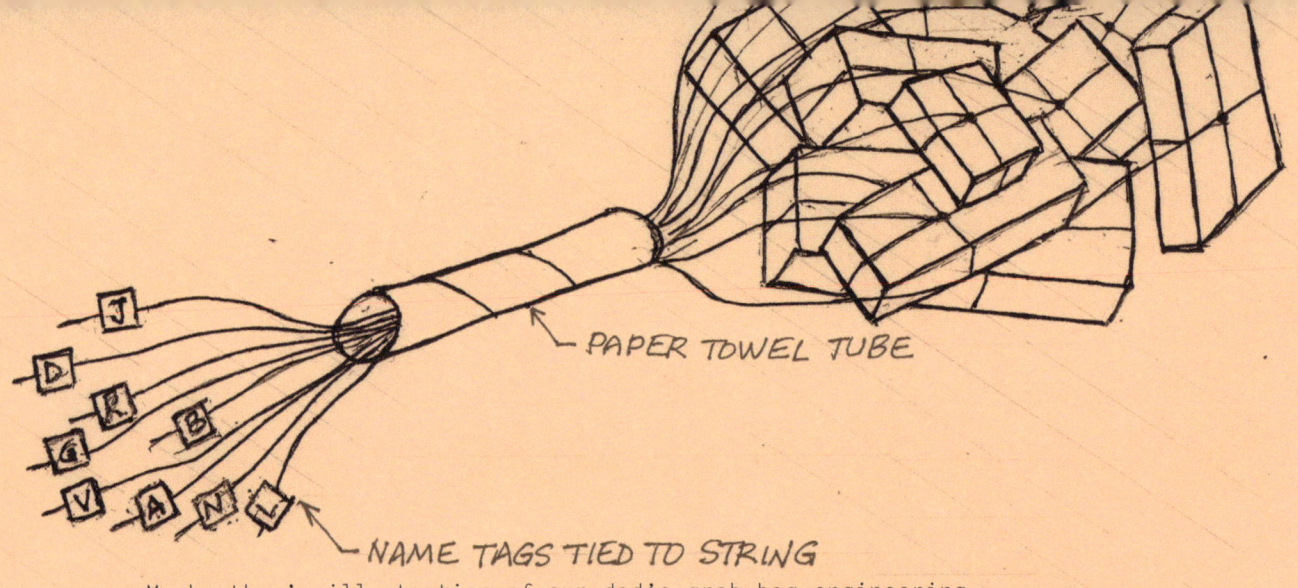

My brother's illustration of our dad's grab-bag engineering

My father, who was probably the greatest agnostic of his generation, turned into Babbo Natale (Santa Claus) on the days leading up to December 24. He would devise all kinds of grab-bag techniques and machinations for distributing his oddball presents purchased at the Odd Lot closeout store on Chambers Street in Manhattan. Each misfit gift was eccentrically wrapped and attached to a long piece of twine labeled with a recipient's name. To sustain suspense, he would snake the twine through a cardboard tube from which we would pull the string. Every Christmas we drew our crazy gifts one by one, trailed by screams of laughter at the sheer uselessness of what we unwrapped. One year, he even wrapped a cooked chicken in a can.

Shopping for the Christmas Eve dinner was, and is, the most revered and strategic part of our ritual. Mom could always be found editting her grocery list from the one she saved from the previous year. Before the hunt swung fully into action, there would have to be the family summit. It was always held at Aunt Jo and Uncle Joe's cozy two-bedroom 600-square-foot apartment over coffee and Ebinger's blackout cake to discuss which fish market had the freshest fish.

They would argue, "Henry's shrimp stunk last year although the baccalà is always the best." "Maybe better to buy them frozen from the new Chinese on 20th Avenue." "Have you tried Sea Breeze?" Why should I go all the way to 85th Street when Henry's is right on 18th and 61st?" Traveling more than a 10-block radius didn't sit well with a family who took "buying local" very seriously.

Left to Right: Sea Breeze II; packing orders; my mom in her kitchen on 61st Street

Standing vigil

Depending on when you arrived at Sea Breeze II, you could expect no less than a 30-minute wait before being waved in by one of the illustrious fishmongers. There was a certain vibe and anticipation waiting on line in the brisk December air. I would often hear "foodie" conversations, comparisons, and advice. No matter the difference in a family's way of preparing the fish feast, we were all on the same chapter. Sound bites of advice filled the time, personal footnotes from relatives: "Grandma made it that way for as long as I can remember." We of the younger generation simply listened, wondering if we would someday have stories of our own.

Unannounced, Angelo would visit his patrons. Swathed in his white, fish-splattered coat and using animated hand gestures, he was always in mid-performance. Angelo was a maestro of the telephone, using it as a 20th-century tracking device and guiding traffic-bound delivery men along the best route from Hunts Point Market. His wife calmly tended to business inside. Being there, waiting and absorbing the energy, reinforced the commitment we all had to tradition.

Mom (second from left) on line at Sea Breeze II, two days before Christmas

My father and Uncle Joe always got a charge from seeing our generation's squeamish reactions to the nightmarish, wiggly creatures that invaded our kitchen sink. After a while, though, the concept of "farm to table" became the norm for us, just as it always had been for them. Marinated anguilla (eel) with mint, garlic, vinegar, and olive oil was one of them. It took me 10 years to get the courage to enjoy this wonderful delicacy.

Above: Fishmonger with a live denizen of the deep, sold during Christmas season. Below: Octopus slowly simmers in tomato sauce.

Insalata di Frutti di Mare

Seafood salad that we wait all year for. Serves 8 to 10.

2 bay leaves
2 pound octopus, cleaned
2 pounds large shrimp, shelled, deveined, and steamed
1 pound lobster tail, steamed, and cut into 1-inch pieces
½ pound scungili cleaned, steamed and cut into ½-inch pieces
1½ pounds squid with tentacles, cleaned, steamed, and cut into ½-inch rings
2 cloves garlic, peeled and crushed, divided
1-2 tablespoons sea salt
Juice from 4-6 lemons (½-¾ cups), divided
3 cups of sliced hearty green celery
1 teaspoon fresh chopped parsley
½ tablespoon freshly ground black pepper
Sea salt to taste
1 cup extra virgin olive oil
Lemons for garnish

Fill a 6-quart pot with water. Add salt and bay leaves and bring to a boil over medium-high heat. Holding the octopus by the head, dip the tentacles quickly in and out of the water 3 times. After the third time, immerse the whole octopus, cover, and boil for 30 minutes. Turn off the heat and leave the octopus in the covered pot of water for another 30 minutes.

Remove the octopus from the water and set it on a board to cool. With a clean towel, wipe off as much of the thin layer of skin as possible. Cut into ½-inch slices.

Rub a large bowl with two cracked cloves of garlic. Place all of the cooled fish in the bowl. Add the salt, half of the lemon juice, the remaining clove of garlic, and mix well. Cover the bowl and place the mixture in the refrigerator to marinate for 12 hours. Stir occasionally.

Remove the mixture from the refrigerator when ready to serve. Remove the cracked garlic clove and discard. Add the celery, parsley, remaining lemon juice, black pepper, and olive oil. Mix well to combine.

Serve on a platter garnished with cut lemons. You will want a yearly invite.

GREETINGS

12-24-87

from CHEZ TWO JO'S
MENU

SEA SALAD

PULPO w/ LINGUINE

FILET OF LEMON SOLE, SMELTS, AND SHRIMPS FRIED TO GOLDEN PERFECTION BY "BIG DADDY"

FRIED PEPPERS ON BACCALA INSALATA

ESCAROLA IN BUTITTA

PICKLED EELS

SCUNGILLI A LA CHEZ TWO JO'S

DESSERT

CAFE NERO   PIZZA DOLCE "NANA"

ASSORTED NUTS + FRUIT

FINOCCHIO, IF WE REMEMBER....

BON APETITE !

Linguine con Sugo di Polipo

Octopus sauce with linguini. Serves 6 to 8.

5 28-ounce cans of plum tomatoes, blended with the juice for 5 seconds
6 tablespoons olive oil, divided
4 cloves of garlic, chopped
1 teaspoon of dried oregano
1 teaspoon dried crushed red chili pepper
8 ounces of dry white wine
3 1- to 1½-pound octopus, cleaned (Spanish octopus preferred)
Sea salt to taste
1-2 pounds dry linguini pasta

Heat 3 tablespoons of olive oil in an 8-quart sauce pot over low heat. Add garlic and sauté until the garlic is light brown. Add the oregano and crushed chili pepper. Cook until there is a red hue to the oil around the pepper flakes. Add the wine and simmer for 1 to 2 minutes, allowing the alcoholto cook off. Stir in the prepared tomatoes, cover, and bring to a boil over medium heat.

While the sauce is boiling, add the octopus by dipping the tentacles in and out of the sauce three times. Then place the entire body into the pot, cover,
and bring back to a boil. Reduce the heat to low and simmer uncovered for 2 to 3 hours or until the octopus is tender and easily pierced with a fork. Season with salt to taste.

In another 6- to 8-quart sauce pot, boil enough water for cooking the pasta. Add 1 tablespoon of salt to the water and cook the pasta until al dente.

Reserve 2 cups of the pasta water before draining the pasta. Return the pasta
to the pot. Add 3 ladles of sauce to the pasta along with some of the pasta water, folding until the pasta is well coated and creamy looking.

Place pasta in a serving bowl, top with sauce, crushed pepper, and a drizzle of olive oil. Serve octopus on a separate platter if preferred.

Note: If you are using only 1 pound of pasta, the remaining sauce will keep well in the freezer for months.

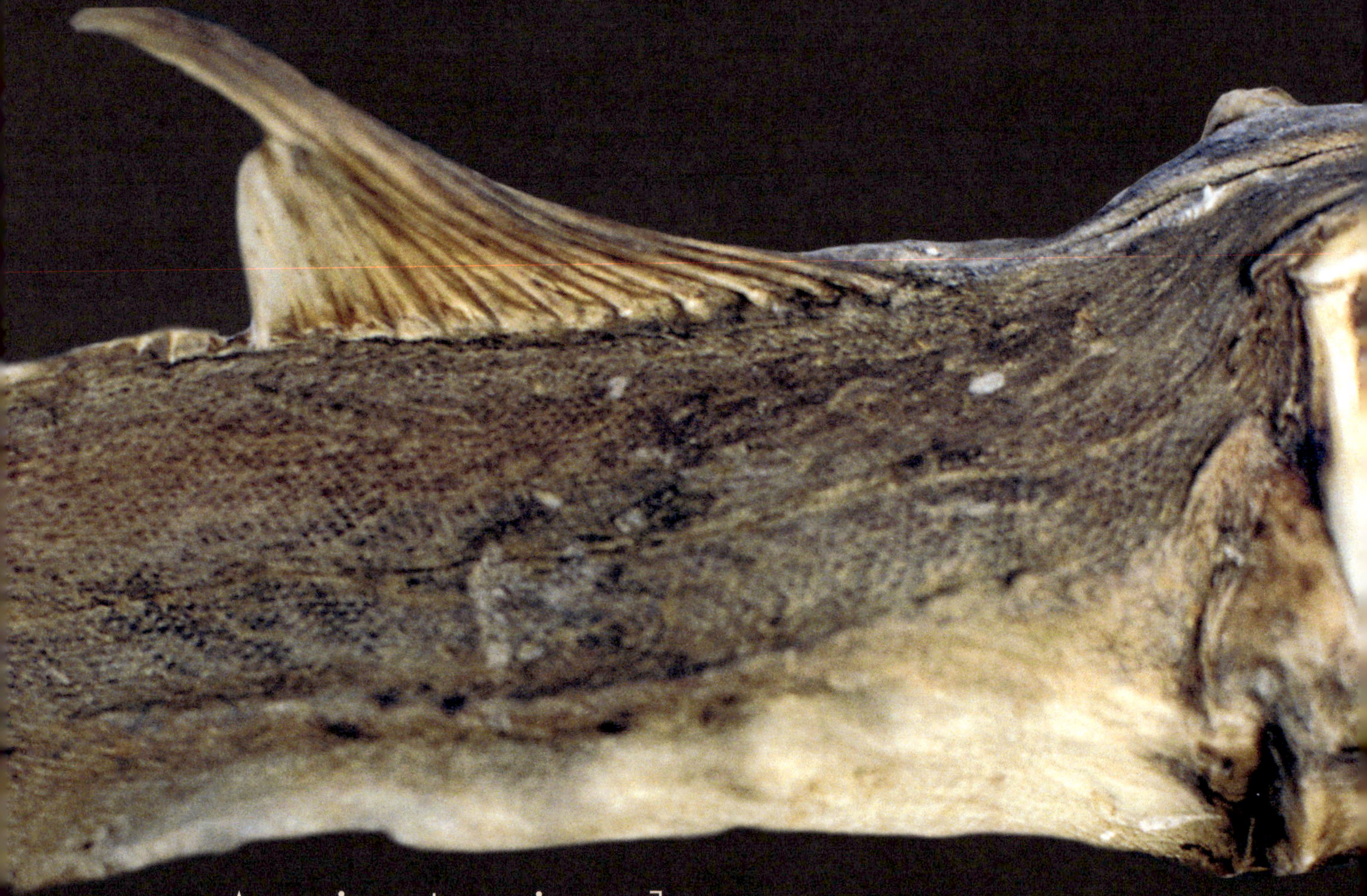

Ancient miracle

Stoccafisso or stocco—turning stone to fish—is a labor-intensive dish that requires Arctic air-dried cod to hydrate for two weeks. Stoccafisso (baked cod) has become an expensive delicacy but it once afforded sustenance to the impoverished.

STOCCO

2 1BS STOCCO ....cut stocco in 2" pieces
3 ONIONS ABOUT (2 or 3) celery sticks & Capers
FLOUR & FRY ..WHILE FRYING COOK SAUCE...lightly saute
AUTE CELERY FIRST TAKE OUT & ADD ONIONS & GARLIC
ONIONS & CELERY...WHEN SAUCE IS ALMOST COOKED, ADD
SOME CAPERS, BLACK & GREEN OLIVES
don't use Red Pack - use only plum tomatoes
PLACE FRIED STOCCO IN BAKING DISH & BAKE FOR ABOUT
(1) HOUR OREGANO - OPTIONAL
USE (1) CAN OF TOMATOS FOR 2LBS OF STOCCO (no paste)
350 OVEN
BEFORE FRYING MAKE SURE SQUEEZE WATER FROM STOCCO
THIS CAN BE PREPARED DAY BEFORE

STOCCO STEW
2 cans tomato..3 onion
5 sticks celery,olives
capers (black & green)

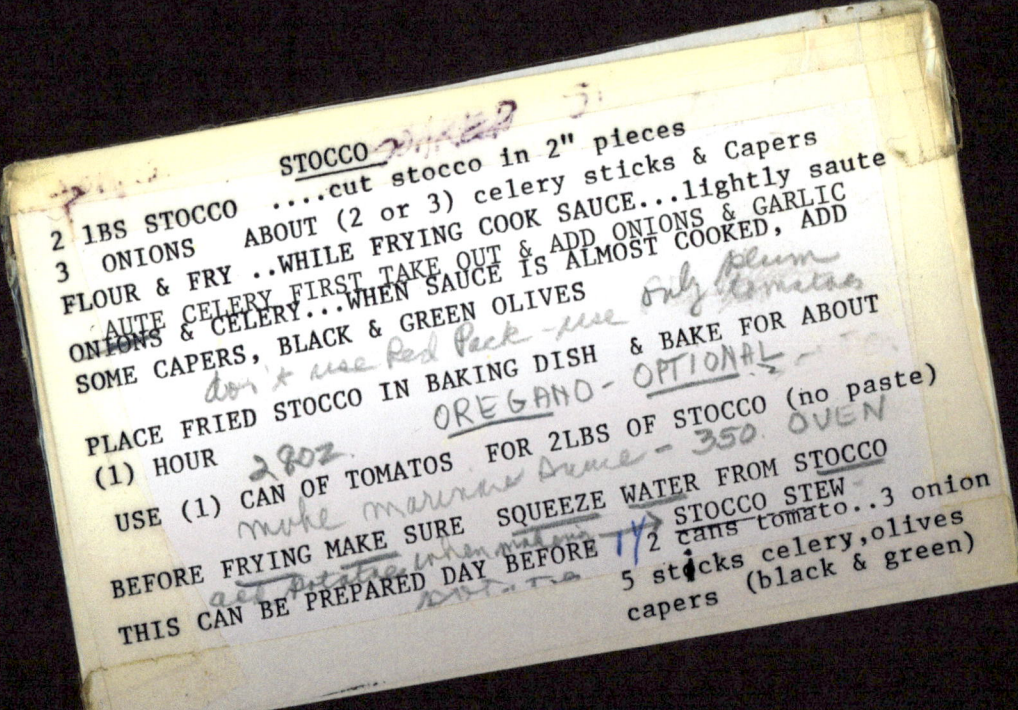

Opposite: My mom's recipe card for hearty stocco al forno. This page: The dish, as mastered by my brother, Robert.

Stoccafisso (Stocco)

Baked codfish, old-school style. Serves 8.

Sauce:
3 pounds of Arctic air-dried cod (stocco)
5 28-ounce cans of Italian plum tomatoes, blended for 4 seconds
3 Spanish onions sliced thin
8-10 stalks of celery, sliced 1-inch on an angle
5 tablespoons salted capers
5 cloves cracked garlic (remove after sauce is cooked)
12 ounces extra-large black pitted olives
12 ounces green Sicilian pitted olives
4 ounces extra virgin olive oil
2 teaspoons salt, more or less to your liking
1 teaspoon of oregano, optional

Fish:
1 cup all-purpose flour
8 ounces canola or corn oil
¼ teaspoon ground black pepper

To make the sauce, add the oil to a 10-quart pot over medium flame. After 1 or 2 minutes add celery and sauté for 5 minutes. Remove and set aside. Add onions and garlic until translucent, remove and set aside. Add blended tomatoes and salt, bring to a boil then lower to simmer uncovered for 45 minutes to 1 hour. After 30 minutes add the sauteed celery, onions and garlic back in, then add the capers and olives. Continue to simmer.

The dry cod must be cut by machine by your merchant into 2-3-inch steaks. Hydrate fish in water for 14 days in your refrigerator, changing water every day. By day 14, your fish will have miraculously turned to flesh. Filet and deboning are optional.

Once fish is ready, preheat oven to 350°F. Heat the canola oil in a medium-sized pan. Flour both sides of each piece of fish while the oil gets hot. Then add the fish to the hot oil. Be careful not to overcrowd the pan, which will slow down frying. Once the fish is light golden brown, remove and set aside to drain excess oil.

Add enough sauce to cover the bottom of a 4½-quart (10-by-15-inch) casserole pan. Add the fried fish to the pan and ladle the tomato sauce over it, covering the fried fish. Bake uncovered in the oven for 45 minutes. Remove from the oven let set for 15 minutes. Serve warm.

The stoccafisso, before and after hydration

Since my father's passing, my brother and I have taken the lead in preparing the family's Christmas Eve dinner. Tectonic life events infuse depth and meaning into family celebrations.

Mom and I would always visit specialty shops—the variety of ingredients required traveling to different stores. What is now considered shopping for "artisanal" ingredients was a way of life. Nowadays, Robert has taken charge of purchasing the stocco, and I have hauled as much as 34 pounds of fish into my mother's fridge on many a December night.

Fritto Misto di Pesce

Mixed fried fish. Serves 6 to 8.

5 cups canola oil
½ cup olive oil
1 cup Wondra flour
2 tablespoons semolina flour
1 teaspoon sea salt
½ pound large shrimp, peeled and deveined
½ pound squid with tentacles, cut into ½-inch rings
½ pound small whiting, sardines, or mullet, cleaned, deboned if the fish
  is mature or large
½ pound smelts, cleaned and deboned
Salt and pepper to taste
Iceberg lettuce or cleaned dry arugula for serving
Lemon wedges for garnish

Pour the canola and olive oil into a 4-quart saucepan and place over medium-high heat. Using a deep-fry thermometer, heat the oil to 350°F. Prepare a cooking sheet or board with a rack, or line with paper towel. Set aside.

Combine both flours and salt in a medium-sized plastic zip-lock bag. Working in batches, place the fish in the bag and toss to coat on all sides. Remove the fish and place on waxed paper until frying.

When the oil has reached 350°F, place some of the floured fish into the oil, taking care not to crowd the pan. Fry the fish about 2 to 3 minutes until it is golden brown. Remove the fish with a slotted spoon and place on the prepared rack or paper towel to drain.

Make sure the oil heats back up to 350°F before adding the next batch of fish. Continue in this manner until all the fish is fried. Season
to taste.

Arrange greens on a large serving platter and place the fish on top of the greens. Serve with lemon wedges.

Insalata di Baccalà e Peperoni

Salt cod with fried peppers is a divine mix of mild salt and sweet caramelized peppers. Serves 8.

2 pounds salt cod, cut into 3-inch pieces
4 pounds red bell peppers, cored and sliced (8 to 9 medium)
3 cloves of garlic, peeled and crushed
4 tablespoons olive oil for frying peppers
1 teaspoon fresh chopped parsley

Rinse cod from initial salt and place it in a container. Fill your container with water to cover fish, cover tightly, and place in the refrigerator. The water should be refreshed at least twice a day for 3 to 4 days to remove salt. (Place your index finger into the center of a piece of the fish, it should not taste overly salty.) After soaking the cod, remove it from the refrigerator and allow it to come to room temperature.

Fill a 6-quart pot with water and bring to a boil over medium-high heat. Add half of the fish to the water and boil it for about 5 minutes or until it looks flaky. Remove the fish from the water with a slotted spoon and place it in a large strainer. Add the remaining pieces of fish to the boiling water and cook in the same manner. Set the strainer with all of the fish aside to cool.

Once the cod is cool enough to handle, remove the bones and as much of the skin as you can. Arrange all of the fish, skin-side down, on a flat platter, cover with wax paper and set aside.

Heat the olive oil in large skillet over medium heat. Add the peppers and garlic and fry until the peppers are tender and begin to caramelize in some areas. Remove from the heat and cool. When the peppers are cooled, remove the wax paper from the platter and spoon them over the fish. Add parsley and serve.

Below: Mom's recipe card with reference to beloved Henry's Fish Market.

<u>BACCALA</u>   2lbs Baccala
3 lbs red peppers...peppers should have a little green on them

BOIL FISH (TAKES JUST A FEW MINUTES TO BOIL) STRAIN FISH VERY WELL ..THEN BREAK UP INTO SMALL PIECES REMOVING ANY BONES. FRY PEPPERS ADD PLENTY OF GARLIC WHEN COOKED POUR (HOT) FRIED PEPPERS <u>IMMEDIATELY</u> ON FISH ..THIS RECEIPE CAN BE PREPARED DAY BEFORE SERVE AT ROOM TEMPETURE

BACCALA CAN BE PREPARED WITH VINEGAR PEPPERS, GARLIC & FRESH PARSLEY.

buy Bacala in Henry's

Leave some room

No matter how stuffed our bellies felt and no matter how long we waited for this dish, scarole ripiene never failed to please. The salty sweet filling of pine nuts, raisins, anchovies, olives, garlic, and cheese made for a family favorite.

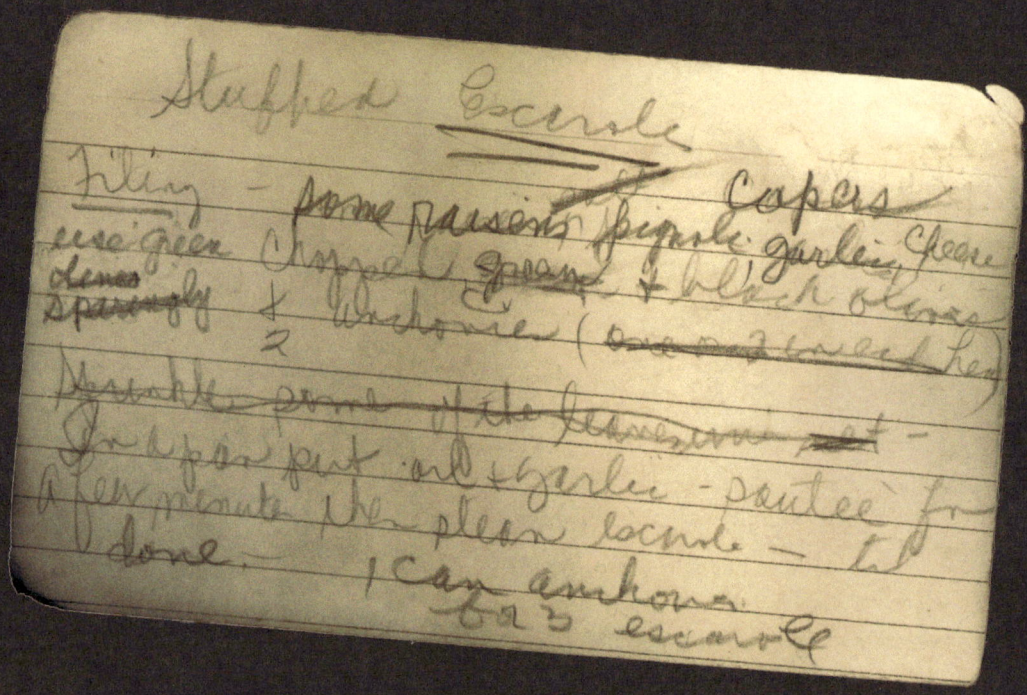

Recipe card for scarole ripiene (stuffed escarole)

I always likened our once-a-year stuffed escarole to an extraordinary wrapped gift

Scarole Ripiene

Stuffed escarole or, in Neapolitan, scarola imbottita. Make extra because it goes quick. Serves 2.

1 medium head escarole

Stuffing:
1 tablespoon pine nuts
1 teaspoon finely chopped garlic
2 slices of salted anchovies in oil
2 tablespoons black raisins
⅛ cup sliced pitted Italian green olives
⅛ cup sliced pitted black olives
1½ tablespoons grated Romano cheese
1 teaspoon salted capers, rinsed well
½ teaspoon freshly ground black pepper
2 tablespoon extra virgin olive oil
2 large garlic cloves, crushed
1 large garlic clove, cracked
18-24 inches of butchers twine for tying

Trim any black or discolored leaf ends from the escararole. Fill a large bowl of fresh water and immerse the head of escarole upside down. Slowly dunk up and down several times to dislodge soil between leaves.

Drain the escarole upside down for about 30 minutes. Once the excess water has drained, carefully remove some of the base at the end of the stalk, making sure the leaves remain attached.

Spread the escarole open so you can see the lighter green center leaves. Mix all of the stuffing ingredients into a bowl and add abound to the center heart of the escarole, gently spreading it flat. Carefully gather all of the leaves to close the escarole back to its natural shape and lay it down on its side.

Make a large slipknot with twine and place it around the escararole, about 3 inches from the base, pulling firmly to close. Continue wrapping the twine tightly around the head in a crisscross pattern until you reach the top. Tie off the twine.

Place the oil in a skillet over low heat. Add the cracked garlic and lightly brown it on both sides. Carefully place the wrapped escarole in the skillet. Cover the skillet and steam the escarole for 25 to 30 minutes or until it is very tender and pierces easily with a fork. Remove the twine, slice in half lengthwise, and serve in a shallow bowl.

Oreganata di Gamberi al Forno

Baked shrimp with lemon and oregano. Serves 8.

18 jumbo shrimp, peeled and deveined with tail left on
¾ cup extra virgin olive oil, divided
2 cups bread crumbs
4 cloves garlic, minced
Juice of 4 lemons (about 4 tablespoons)
1½ tablespoon dried oregano
1 teaspoon fine sea salt
1 teaspoon freshly ground black pepper
2 lemons, quartered for serving

Heat oven to 400°F and prepare top rack.

Using a small paring knife, butterfly the shrimp from the back side. Place 1-2 tablespoons of olive oil in a medium bowl, add the shrimp and toss well to coat. Place butterflied shrimp on a flat cookie sheet.

Using the same bowl, combine the bread crumbs, garlic, lemon juice, oregano, remaining olive oil, salt, and pepper. Mix thoroughly. Spoon about 1½ tablespoons of bread crumb mixture onto the flattened shrimp, shaping it into a small mound.

Place the cookie sheet into the preheated oven for no more than 8 or 10 minutes, or until the shrimp are opaque or bread crumbs are golden brown. Serve with freshly squeezed lemon juice.

Tip: When cooking fish or any meat, remove it from refrigeration in advance of cooking. It will make the cooking time more accurate.

Anguilla Fritta con la Menta

Fried eel with mint and white balsamic vinegar. Serves 4 to 6.

¼ cup olive oil for frying
1 small eel, cleaned by fishmonger, at room temperature
1 cup of all-purpose flour
1 teaspoon of ground sea salt, divided
½ cup white wine vinegar
Fresh ground black pepper to taste
2 tablespoons extra virgin olive oil, more to drizzle over eel
Fresh sprigs of Italian mint

Place a cast iron skillet over medium-low heat and add the olive oil. While the oil is heating, pat the eel dry and cut into 2-inch pieces.

Place flour and ½ teaspoon of salt in a paper bag. Add a few pieces of eel at a time to the bag and shake until the pieces are evenly coated on all sides.

Working in batches, put a few pieces of the floured eel into the hot oil, taking care not to crowd the pan. Fry the eel for about 3 to 5 minutes on each side, until it is cooked through and golden brown. Remove the eel from the pan using a slotted spoon, and set aside to cool. Make sure the oil returns to temperature before adding the next batch. Continue in this manner until all the eel is fried.

Combine the vinegar, ½ teaspoon of salt, black pepper, and extra virgin olive oil in a medium bowl. Add the cooled eel to the bowl and toss gently.

Arrange a bed of fresh mint on a flat platter. Place the eel on top of the mint. Add additional vinegar, oil, salt, and pepper to your taste.

This dish should not be overlooked as it is so succulent.

The last of the dishes for the Feast of the Seven Fishes—scungilli served over friselle, covered with a tomato paste and onion sauce—arrived from the kitchen as late as 10 o'clock, depending on how long it took the children to open Christmas gifts. Opening presents was a brilliant tactic for giving the young ones a break from sitting at the dinner table as the night carried on. While we occupied ourselves with gifts, clean dishes were returned to the table and dining soon resumed without a hitch.

When we grew older, this final dish was served as we played cards to pass time while Mom sang at midnight Mass. Coffee and dessert was served upon her return at 2:00 a.m. It took the family a while to adjust after my mother committed to leaving her apron behind in pursuit of her passion for singing.

Scungilli con Friselle

Conch with chili sauce over black pepper biscuits. Serves 6.

2 tablespoons extra virgin olive oil
1 small to medium-sized onion, peeled and left whole
1 teaspoon dry oregano
2 teaspoons crushed red chili pepper
18 ounces tomato paste
1 tablespoon sea salt
12 ounces water
2 pounds scungilli, cleaned and thinly sliced
½ pound friselle, black pepper hard biscuits (at Italian bakeries)
Fresh parsley, rough chopped for garnish

Heat the oil in a 2-quart saucepan over low heat. Add the whole onion and cook for about 30 minutes, rotating it around like a ball until all sides are browned, being careful not to burn.

Once all sides are browned, add the oregano and crushed red pepper. Steep until there is a red hue to the oil around the pepper flakes. Add the tomato paste, salt, and water. Cover and simmer over low heat for 1½ hours. Add more salt to your taste.

Fill another 2-quart saucepan with water and bring to a boil. Add the scungilli and reduce heat to a simmer for no more than 5 minutes. These come already cooked so remember you are simply heating them up.

Arrange the biscuits (friselle) on a shallow platter. When the scungilli is cooked, moisten the biscuits with a little of the cooking water. Remove the scungilli from the saucepan using a slotted spoon, and place it on the biscuits. Ladle the sauce over the top, sprinkle with the fresh parsley and serve.

A dish like this made the original Vincent's of Little Italy famous.

Being the youngest somehow equated to getting the worst seat at the table. I recall sitting at the kids' folding table, pretzelling myself into my stool like a contortionist and straddling the table corner while my aunt's starched white tablecloth chafed my chin. Year by year I grew in stature and seniority, and before long I would play cards or go to midnight Mass where I operated a RadioShack Realistic tape deck to record my mom's church choir at Regina Pacis Church.

Above: Christmas Eve with extended family at grandma's house. Below, left to right: My wife, Audra, lighting the candles; Madeline, Luca, and Audra.

SWEET PIE

(handwritten annotations: 2 8" pans OR / 9" pan good / 350-375 for 1 hr. 45 min / Italian cheese cake / 3 lbs ricotta)

CRUST (Pasta frolla)   DOUBLE RECEIPT FOR 3 PIES

2 CUPS OF SIFTED FLOUR
1/2 CUP OF SOFT BUTTER
2 EGGS
1 CUP SUGAR — 3/4 to 1 cup
1/2 TEA. GRATED LEMON RIND

SIFT TOGETHER FLOUR, SUGAR & SALT, MAKE A WELL OF DRY INGREDIENTS ON PASTRY BOARD, PLACE EGGS, LEMON RIND IN WELL AND WORK DOUGH WITH HANDS...DO NOT ADD WATER. WHEN SMOOTH SHAPE INTO BALL AND CHILL FOR 30 MINUTES AND THEN ROLL OUT. PIECE THE DOUGH BECAUSE DOUGH IS SOFT AND FALLS APART.

When making Italian cheese cake you can add 1 pt. heavy cream

My mom's recipe card for torta dolce—always a sweet send-off to a fabulous Christmas Eve

Torta Dolce di Ricotta

After fruit, chestnuts, and presents had been handed out, there was always room for the only dessert on the menu: torta dolce (sweet pie). This traditional cheesecake (without cream cheese) has the perfect blend of sugary citrus, creamy yet almost flaky ricotta, and a refreshing hint of anise. No one left the house without it. A pie serves 10 to 12.

Crust:
2 cups all-purpose flour, plus extra to dust board and pan
¾ cup sugar
Zest of one lemon
½ cup unsalted butter, softened, plus extra to grease the pan
2 large eggs

Filling:
8 large eggs
3 pounds ricotta cheese, drained of excess water
2 teaspoons vanilla
1½ cups sugar
Zest of 2 oranges
Juice of 1 orange
Juice of 1 lemon
¼ cup candied pear, chopped, optional

To make the crust, place the flour, sugar, and zest on a pastry board or clean, dry flat surface. Mix thoroughly to combine. Add the butter and work it into the dry ingredients. Gather the mixture into a mound and create a well in the center. Refrigerate for 30 minutes.

Preheat oven to 350°F. Butter and flour a 10-inch springform baking pan. Set aside.

Meanwhile, to prepare the filling, combine the eggs, ricotta cheese, vanilla, sugar, orange zest, orange juice, lemon juice, and candied pear (if using) in a large mixing bowl. Mix thoroughly and set aside.

After the 30 minutes, remove the dough from the refrigerator and place it on a large board or clean, dry flat surface, lightly dusted with flour. Using a floured rolling pin, roll the dough out into a large circle, approximately 14 inches in diameter. Now roll the dough over the rolling pin and carefully unwind it over the baking pan, gently easing it to fit evenly in the bottom and up the sides of the pan.

Pour or spoon the filling mixture into the crust, leaving about ¼ inch below the rim of the pan. Place the pan in a preheated oven and bake for 1 hour and 45 minutes, until the center is slightly firm. Cool for at least 2 hours. I have left it unrefrigerated overnight when I have baked it the night before to save time.

Carefully run a plastic knife or rigid spatula around the sides of pan to remove it, so that no crust is pulled away when you release the spring of the pan. Serve at room temperature.

Christmas Day
The Christmas Day Menu

Antipasti
Artichoke
Lasagne
Braciole
Meatballs
Sausages
Struffoli

Christmas Mass at Regina Pacis church, 65th Street, Brooklyn. My mother (middle row, second from right) and her choir featured in the *The New York Times's Sunday Magazine*, December 1967.

Antipasti

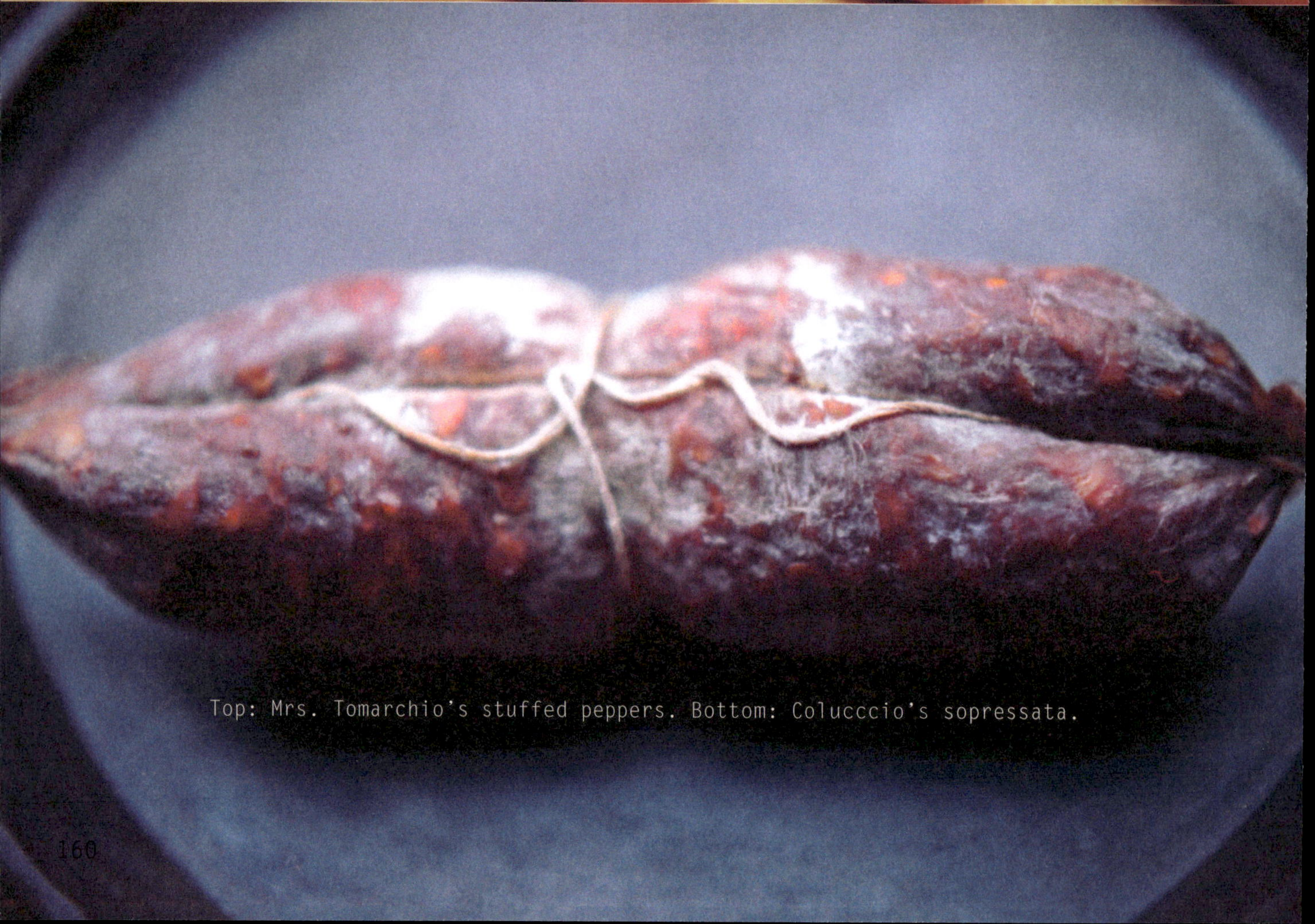

Top: Mrs. Tomarchio's stuffed peppers. Bottom: Colucccio's sopressata.

Carciofi Ripieni

Artichokes can be stuffed with seasoned bread crumbs or simply with garlic and fresh parsley. Serves 5.

5 medium cleaned and cored artichokes. Choose artichokes that are more squat rather than cone shaped. If the artichoke is fresh it will squeak when you squeeze them.

Bread stuffing:
4 cups bread crumbs
½ cup Romano cheese
2 cloves garlic, chopped
1 cups olive oil
1 tsp black pepper
Juice from one lemon
1 teaspoon oregano
1 teaspoon salt, or to your taste

Simple stuffing:
6 tablespoons fresh parsley
5 cloves garlic, halved
1 teaspoon salt, or to your taste

Cooking:
2 tablespoons extra olive oil
2 cloves garlic, cracked
3 cups water

Combine above ingredients in a small bowl for either style stuffing.

Discard some of the tougher outer leaves of the artichoke, at least two exterior rows. Cut of the tips of the leaves (it looks fancier) with kitchen scissors or take a serrated knife across the tops. Cut the stem down so the artichoke can sit without toppling over. The stems are tender when cooked as well, but be sure to peel the outer layer of skin off.

Begin to loosen the center by spreading the leaves outward with your thumbs to create a pocket to add stuffing. Using a teaspoon, remove the choke by spreading the leaves, grabbing the center part between the spoon and your thumb, and removing all of the fibers. Stuff inside the pocket you created with the ingredients and set aside.

Add the oil and garlic to a large-enough pan over a low flame, and sauté until golden brown. Place the artichokes in the pan carefully, then add water. Cover and steam for at least one hour or until a leaf can be easily pulled off. Spoon the broth from the pan back on top of each choke and serve warm.

Above: The table set for Christmas. Below: My father's favorite way of presenting antipasti.

Antipasto translates to "before the meal." This is the traditional appetizer course of any formal Italian meal, especially on Christmas and Easter. Typically antipasti include cured meats, olives, peperoncini, mushrooms, anchovies, and artichoke hearts, plus a wealth of cheeses and vegetables.

Mrs. Tomarchio's Stuffed Peppers Sotto Olio
Fills 4 to 5 12-ounce Ball jars.

16 fresh hot cherry peppers, seeds and core removed
16 ounces white vinegar

Stuffing:
4 cups bread crumbs
6-8 salted anchovies, minced then pureed
2 cups olive oil
½ cup grated Romano cheese
1 teaspoon freshly ground black pepper
1 teaspoon sea salt
4-5 12-ounce Ball canning jars
Olive oil
4-5 dried bay leaves

Bring 16 ounces of water and 16 ounces of white vinegar to a boil in a medium saucepan over medium-high heat. Add the peppers and parboil them for 2 minutes. Remove the peppers from the pan with a slotted spoon and set aside to cool.

Combine the bread crumbs, anchovies, oil, cheese, pepper, and salt in a large mixing bowl.

Once the peppers are cool enough to handle, scoop the bread crumb mixture into each pepper, patting down until solid and filled to the rim of the pepper. Stack the stuffed peppers into each jar, leaving space to top off with enough olive oil to cover the peppers. Add a dry bay leaf to each jar and seal. Use within three months. Refrigerate after two months to keep longer.

Mrs. Barletta's Marinated Eggplant Sotto Olio
Fills 4 to 5 12-ounce Ball jars.

Sea salt
1 cup apple cider or white wine vinegar
1 tablespoon dry oregano
Freshly ground black pepper
2 celery stalks, cut into ⅛-inch slices
2 cloves garlic, minced
4-5 fresh sprigs of oregano
4-5 12-ounce Ball canning jars
Olive oil

Slice each eggplant into strips, ½-inch thick by 2-inches long. Sprinkle the strips generously with salt, place them in a colander, and cover with a plate. Add a weight, pressing down to help drain the eggplant. Let stand for two hours and wipe dry after draining.

After the eggplant has drained, place the strips into a bowl and add the vinegar and dry oregano. Add salt and black pepper to taste. Marinate the eggplant for one hour at room temperature.

Mix in the celery and garlic after the eggplant has marinated. Fill the jars with eggplant mixture to 1½ inches below the top. Place one sprig of oregano in the side of each jar. Top off with olive oil, making sure to cover the ingredients so nothing is above the oil. Use within three months. Refrigerate after two months to keep longer.

Mrs. Tomarchio's stuffed peppers. I met her son John when I was living in Boston's North End. Judging from the energy in his voice, I knew he was from my Brooklyn neighborhood. Turns out, his mom still lived three blocks from my childhood home and we have been fast friends ever since.

Mrs. Barletta's marinated eggplant. Originally from Baci, Mrs. Barletta was a neighbor of ours. A recent arrival from Italy, she was taken under my grandmother's wing. My mother also helped her gain a foothold by setting up her first bank account.

Tomato Sauce Fundamentals

My family's general—and subjective—rule was as follows: If the mixture had a meat component and was made on a holiday or a Sunday afternoon, we referred to it as gravy. Anything else was plain tomato sauce.

Gravy for the Christmas meal was always prepared the night before and refrigerated. This ensured a small break from cooking, or from cooking quite as much on Christmas. The added benefit was the fact the overnight wait also developed a richer taste.

Redpack plum tomatoes were usually my mom's preferred choice until, the San Marzano type became popular in the 1970s. Today, I enjoy seeing so many beautiful labels and brands. My favorites are Pastosa, Coluccio, and Marinella tomatoes, not simply for their great taste, but also because of the lining of their cans. Each can has an enameled coating thus eliminating the sometimes canned taste.

These recipes for tomato sauce are general guides, as I know them. They change depending on where in Italy your family originated. As you travel north of Rome, less garlic is used. If the tomatoes you use taste acidic, try adding ¼ teaspoon or less baking soda to neutralize the acidity.

Marinara sauce:
The root word "mare" translates to "sea." Always good to have on hand, this sauce was traditionally made by fishermen and was meant to be thrown together quickly. The only spice they used was a pinch of dry oregano or hint of anchovies. Traditionally used when cooking fish—especially shellfish. A modified version with finely chopped garlic is intended for those who like a bolder flavor.

2 28-ounce cans of plum tomatoes (puree for 3 to 5 seconds)
2 cracked cloves of garlic, if desired
1 teaspoon of salt, or to your taste
¼ cup olive oil
¼ teaspoon dry oregano (or basil)
¼ teaspoon crushed red pepper (ground black pepper substitute)

Brown the garlic in olive oil for about 2 to 5 minutes over a low flame until golden brown. Add the oregano or basil and stir until wilted. Add tomatoes and stir. Bring to boil, then simmer on low for 20 to 30 minutes. Turn off heat.

Tomato sauce with onion:
Same as above but with the addition of finely chopped sweet onion. Used when preparing baked dishes or cooking with meat and for stews. After the garlic has browned, cook the onions in olive oil for about 2 to 3 minutes over a low flame until translucent. Add the basil and stir until wilted. Add tomatoes and stir. Bring to boil then simmer on low for 20 to 30 minutes. Turn off the heat.

Simple meat sauce:
Start by browning the meat—a combination of the following is traditional: meatballs, ribs, or braciole. Remove the meat from the pan, and add the garlic and onion to the pan. Fry until the onion is translucent. Add ¼ cup of red wine to liquify all that has caramelized in the pot. Add the 28 ounces of pureed tomatoes, then return the browned meat to the pot. Simmer for 2 to 3 hours.

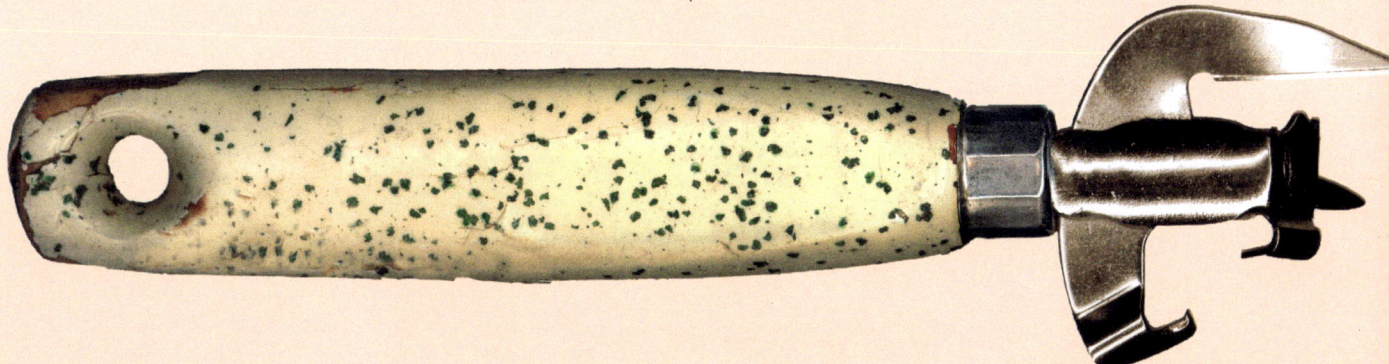

My grandmother's hand can opener from the 1940s. I use it to demonstrate to our children that good ideas that worked then still work today.

Meat Sauce Essentials

Olive oil
Garlic
Tomato sauce
Red wine
Braciole
Meat balls
Pork ribs
Sausage
Tomatoes

Hallelujah for meat sauce and the glow of good old analog Christmas lights

Christmas Day Sauce

We always called it "the gravy."

8-9 28-ounce cans of whole tomatoes
  (blended each for 3 to 5 seconds)
10 cloves of garlic, finely sliced
8 teaspoons salt, or to your taste
2 cups olive oil
1 pound hot sausage
1 pound sweet sausage
4 pork ribs or chops
1 beef braciola
1 pork braciola
10-12 meatballs
1 cup red wine

After the sausage, ribs, braciole, and meatballs have been browned and removed from the sauté pot, turn the heat to medium-low and add the sliced garlic. Keeping a bottle of red table wine at hand, sauté garlic until golden brown.

As the garlic reaches color, quickly add the red wine and simmer for 5 minutes, mixing in all the wonderful pan juices from the sautéed meat. Add browned meat, then the tomatoes.

Cover the pot and bring to boil. Turn heat to low and simmer uncovered for no less than four hours. Remove meatballs after 1½ hours and remove braciole when tender. Judge by piercing—it's ready when it's easy to pierce the braciola with a sharply pointed fork.

Braciola

The secret ingredient to my meat sauce is the pork and beef braciole. It provides the essence of the sauce's flavor. Braciole can be served as a stand-alone dish on regular days, but when added to the gravy, they infuse the sauce with a decadent richness. Third to the pork and beef versions is a pig skin (cotica) version. Sadly, when big pharma kept lowering "normal" cholesterol levels, this version quickly disappeared from our menu. It will still, thankfully, always show up on Christmas. I can still hear my Aunt Jo saying: "Live it up. You only live once!" Each braciola serves about 4. (Ask the butcher to pound the meat thin.)

1 beef round or flank steak or pork shoulder cut flattened
2½ cups of meat sauce, see page 167
1 clove garlic, minced
2 cups fresh parsley, snipped
1 tablespoon raisins
1 tablespoon pine nuts
1 tablespoon freshly grated pecorino Romano cheese
½ teaspoon freshly ground black pepper
Extra virgin olive oil

Lay the meat out flat on a clean, dry surface. Evenly spread the garlic, parsley, raisins, pine nuts, grated cheese, and black pepper over the steak.

Drizzle 1 tablespoon of extra virgin olive oil over the mixture to moisten. Beginning at one long end, roll the meat firmly—but not too tightly—jelly-roll style. Using cooking twine, make a slipknot over one end to secure the roll. Wind the twine around across the middle to the other end of the roll, then wind it back around crisscrossing the twine to where you started. Then spread back over the center, pressing finger down on twine against cutting board as you change directions.

Heat 2 tablespoons of olive over medium-high heat in a skillet large enough to hold the braciola. Brown the roll on all sides without cooking through. Add the tomato sauce back into your pot if you are making a big pot of "Sunday sauce." Cook for at least 1½ hours or until fork tender.

To serve, remove the braciola from the sauce and place it on a cutting board, allowing it to rest. Remove the twine, cut into six slices and arrange on a platter on a bed of sauce.

The key for any Italian American family is to somehow start cooking for Christmas Day while preparing the Seven Fishes dinner days before. (Thank the Lord for small miracles!)

It's crucial to purchase provisions the day before Christmas Eve. The trick to enjoying the Eve is knowing that almost 200 tedious tiny meatballs (the way the Paternas do it!) have already been prepared and fried.

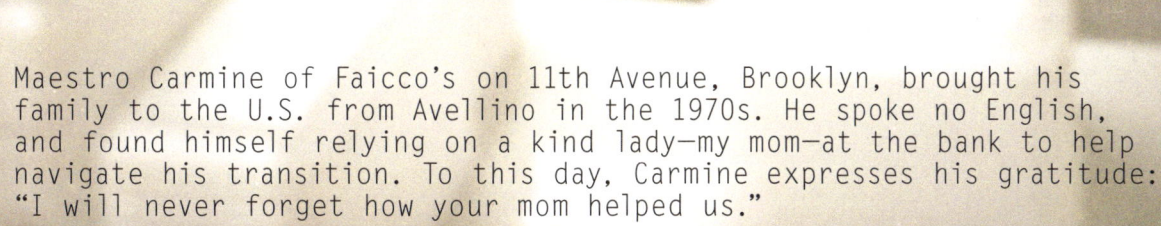

Maestro Carmine of Faicco's on 11th Avenue, Brooklyn, brought his family to the U.S. from Avellino in the 1970s. He spoke no English, and found himself relying on a kind lady—my mom—at the bank to help navigate his transition. To this day, Carmine expresses his gratitude: "I will never forget how your mom helped us."

Italian Americans all over the country would agree on our shared love of meatballs. On any given Sunday, growing up, I would wake up to the wafting essence of fried meatballs weaving its way from the kitchen.

Like clockwork, my father would pinch one of the polpette and eat it, still warm from the frying pan, before they went into the simmering sauce. I can hear him say, "Someday I'd like to sell these out of a pushcart on the street. People would love them!"

Was my father's idea a precursor to the trend-setting food trucks of today? Maybe. Mostly, it was pride in the age-old ritual established every Sunday in Mom's kitchen, and in her diligence in bestowing this tradition upon the next generation.

Two recipe cards for polpette fritte: Aunt Jo's recipe (left) and Mom's recipe (right). Mom was so diligent she credited her sister-in-law by adding her name to the card.

Above: My parents, James and Anne, at a wedding in 1952, one year after their marriage. Below: Our own children 60 years later, enjoying the life my parents strived to give them.

 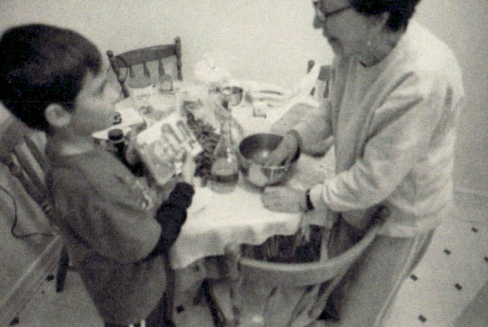 

Polpette

Meatballs have been a fire starter of family discussions (and arguments) for years. I still strive to recreate my mother's perfection. As my cousin Patty states, "I never said this, but your mom's are the best!" Each polpetta is about 2 inches in diameter. Makes 10 to 12 meatballs, to be used in gravy.

½ cup rehydrated Italian bread or bread crumbs
1 pound ground beef
2 eggs
2 cloves garlic, finely chopped
½ cup cold water or milk
½ cup fresh parsley, chopped
½ cup raisins
½ cup grated Romano cheese
1 teaspoon freshly ground black pepper
1 teaspoon sea salt
1 cup flour
1 cup olive oil for frying

Place the rehydrated bread, beef, eggs, garlic, water or milk, parsley, raisins, cheese, pepper, and salt in a large bowl, big enough to use your hands for mixing. Work the ingredients together until you have a consistent texture.

Before rolling the polpette, place the flour in a shallow dish for dredging the meatballs. Use a little of the flour to dust a large flat plate and set both aside.

Dampen your hands using one hand to sprinkle the palm of the other with some water to keep the mixture from sticking. Take approximately ⅓ cup of the mixture in one palm and roll into a ball using both palms, gently compressing the mixture as you roll. Lightly dredge the round ball in flour and set aside on the prepared plate.

While some meatballs are frying, roll another batch. Pour the olive oil into a medium saucepan or large skillet, over medium heat. The bottom of the pan should be well coated. Heat until you see subtle waves along the top of the oil, generally a good indicator that your oil is ready for frying.

Gently lower the dredged meatballs into the oil, rolling each as you place it in the pot. Rotate the meatballs as they cook, using a wide shallow spoon. Make sure to scrape against the pot under the meatball, to keep them from sticking.

Remove the polpette from the oil when they are browned on all sides and place them in a bowl. Set aside. You will add these later to the simmering sauce.

This page: My grandmother's age-old butchering knife. Opposite: The very first food-prep job I had at the age of seven was to stand on a chair and grate cheese using this very 1950s A.S. cheese grater.

Below: Left to right, Aunt Jo; Cousin Livia; Grandpa Giacomo; my father; my Uncle Daniel's British "war bride," Aunt Joan; my mom—sharing a festive meal in the early 1950s. Bottom: My mother's lasagne recipe.

One reason we didn't go out was because spending money to dine out was taken very seriously. Another reason was that a home-cooked meal was always better, especially for any friends lucky enough to be a guest. For those guests, it would be like sitting at a fine restaurant.

On the occasion my family, grandma included, did go out in celebration of any number of sacred events, we made sure to order a special dish we might not often get at home. Lasagne was rarely one of them.

```
              LASAGNE                  BAKE  1 HOUR 3
                                            350 OVEN  375
    2 LBS.  LASAGNA         COOL SAUCE BEFORE MAKING
    3 1/4 lbs. ricotta   --- 1-1/4 LBS. MOZZARELLA    LASAGNA
    1-1/4 LBS   CHOP MEAT FOR SMALL MEAT BALLS.
 slightly                                      over →
    UNDER COOK LASAGNE - OVER LAP LASAGNE SO THAT RICOTTA
    WON'T COME OUT  WHEN SLICING PORTIONS ...SPOON RICOTTA
    ON LASAGNA.....(9) STRIPS FOR EACH LAYER
    USE NO SAUCE OR VERY LITTLE SAUCE ON  TOP LAYER COVER
    WITH FOIL & BAKE
                   Large cans 35 oz.
    USE (3) CANS OF TOMATO AND  ONE PASTE, COOL SAUCE
    BEFORE  USING IT    OR 6 SMALL CANS ( 1 lb. 16 oz.) &
    ONE PASTE   (or)                     PASTE
    LIFT CORNERS OF  FOIL SO THAT CORNERS GET CRUSTY (option
```

Lasagne is a dish that has inspired hundreds of different interpretations; a dish as indigenous to an individual family as their surname. Ordering lasagne out is uncharted territory, even at historic Italian eateries such as The Carolina or Gargiulo's in Coney Island. So, unless you are more open-minded than my parents, you might find you would have been happier eating at home!

The flip side of the lasagne recipe card is a simple diagram my mother sketched out as a reminder to lay the next layer at a 90-degree angle to the previous layer.

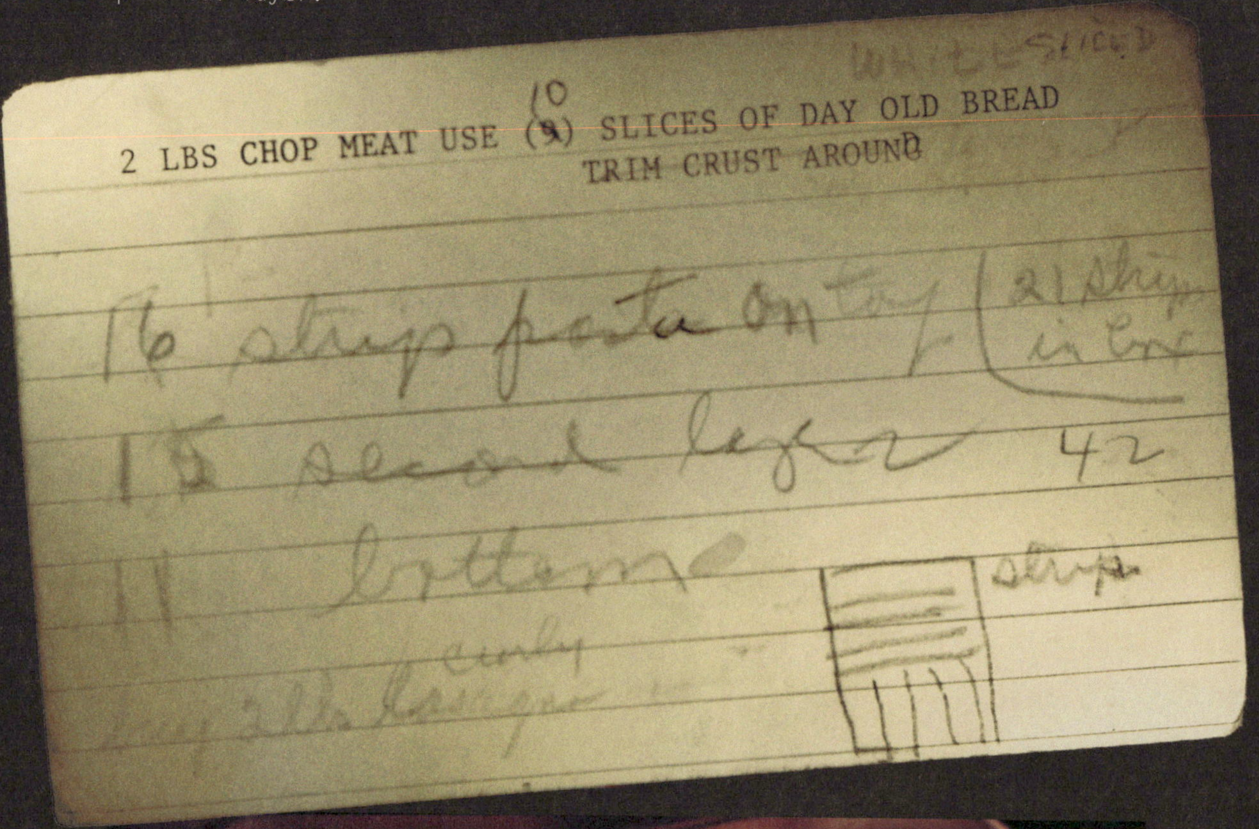

Laying out the pasta sheets in assembling the lasagne. The first layer is laid out lengthwise on the bottom of a rectangular pan. The filling is added and the next layer of pasta sheets is laid perpendicular to the previous.

While dining out, even my father would ocassionally give in to
tempation and order lasagne. After his questions had been answered
by the waiter, he would place his order reluctantly. He would give
restaurant lasagne another try, and inevitably be disappointed.

My dad holding my brother and me, Christmas Eve, 1959.
In the background is our modest Lionel train set under the tree.

A great example of the ultimate gathering—a double wedding at Villa Joe's in Coney Island, 1950. My mom and dad are far left at the foreground table.

Our parents, despite being first—and second-generation immigrants from Campania, Italy, transitioned to modernization and embraced the *cultura americana*. After we had all watched The Beatles' debut on *The Ed Sullivan Show*, Mom gave us Fab Four haircuts. Later, we sported trendy Nehru shirts at family events in the early 1970s.

Despite the clash of old and new cultures, my parents always emphasized the importance of simple culinary delights rooted in our traditional dishes. And why not? When prepared thoughtfully, the results seemed touched by divinity. Some dishes were prefaced with descriptors like "the king of" or "the best of." In this case, as far as my father was concerned, our family made the best lasagne.

According to the master chefs of the household, a lasagna should not appear flat, as when the top layers slide off the layer below. That means there is too much sauce.

I remember the aches from standing around the kitchen table with my cousins, rolling 250 tiny meatballs from the 2-pound mixture of beef, garlic, cheese, rehydrated bread, and parsley. Under my mother's tutelage and my father's watchful eye, we quickly learned that goofing around during these indoctrinating lessons was definitely not part of the process. It was serious business.

Today, our two children help prepare the same Christmas Day lasagne my family has been making for decades. The recipe has survived like an ancient Roman structure. It is uninfluenced by decades of passing gastronomic trends.

Lasagne alla Paterna
Lasagne with tiny meatballs. Serves 14 to 16.

Small meatballs or *polpettine*:
1½ pounds chopped beef
2 medium eggs
1 cup fresh or dry parsley
¾ cup grated Romano cheese
2-3 cloves fresh garlic, finely minced
1 teaspoon black pepper
Salt to taste
16 ounces canola oil for frying

Place the beef, eggs, parsley, cheese, garlic, pepper, and salt in a large bowl. Mix until all of the ingredients are well combined. Dampen your hands and roll the mixture into tiny ¾-inch meatballs. It should yield 150 to 200 meatballs. (It sounds like a lot, but whatever I don't use I save for soup for another day.)

Heat the oil in a large pan over medium heat. When the oil is hot, fry a few meatballs at a time until they are deep golden brown. Remove from the oil and drain the meatballs on paper towels. Cool and set aside.

Lasagne:
4 tablespoons olive oil
2 tablespoons sea salt
2 pounds dry lasagne pasta
3-4 quarts of tomato or meat sauce (page 167)
2 pounds ricotta, drained of excess water
1 pound mozzarella cheese or toma cheese, cut into 1-inch cubes
1½ cups grated Romano cheese
1 cup fresh basil
1 tablespoon black pepper

Preheat oven to 375°F.

Boil 6 quarts of water in an 8-quart pot. Add the olive oil and salt. Place lasagne strips in the water at 90-degree angles, and boil about 5-6 minutes until they bend easily without breaking. Carefully pull the pasta out and drape the strips over the edge of a large, cool pot to drain.

Add enough sauce to cover the bottom of a 4½-quart (10"x 15") casserole pan. Place a layer of lasagne strips, overlapping as you go, to cover the bottom of the pan. Top the pasta with dollops of the ricotta, and some of the cubed mozzarella, grated cheese, polpettine, and basil. Then add two ladles (about 2 cups) of sauce. Continue in this manner with two more layers, placing each layer of pasta at a 90-degree angle to the layers below. Gently press down after each layer. You should get four layers. Finish off with sauce only and cover with a foil tent.

Bake in a preheated oven for 45 minutes to 1 hour or until hot. Remove the pan from the oven and allow the lasagne to settle for 20 to 30 minutes. Cut into squares. Plate and serve with added sauce, grated cheese, or crushed red pepper.

Struffoli

As a rule, *struffoli*—a crusty, honey soaked, Neapolitan dessert flavored with tangerine zest—were made a week in advance of the holiday. My aunts and cousins would descend into my grandmother's kitchen on a school night, roll up their sleeves, and drink lots of coffee to stay awake. The best part was how homework became of secondary importance to rolling and cutting pounds of dough into tiny marble-sized balls. It's a true harbinger of Christmas. Serves 8.

10 large-size egg yolks and 2 egg whites
2 teaspoon baking powder
1¾ pounds unbleached all-purpose flour (approximately 6 cups), plus more for dusting
8 cups honey
3 ounces anisette
4 ounces tangerine or orange juice
4 tangerines or oranges, rinds only (without the pith), sliced very thin
4 cups canola oil for frying

Prepare several baking sheets or platters, half of them with a light dusting of flour, the other half lined with paper towel. Set aside.

Place the egg yolks and whites in a large mixing bowl and beat well. Add the baking powder to the eggs. Gradually add the flour, combining it with the egg until you can knead it into a smooth dough.

Turn the dough out onto a lightly floured, large cutting board or clean, dry, flat surface, Break off a piece of the dough, roll it into a long ½-inch diameter strand and cut the strand into ¾-inch pieces. With floured hands, roll each piece into a ball and place on the prepared cookie sheet or platter. Continue in this manner until all of the dough has been rolled into balls.

Heat the oil in a 6-quart pot over medium heat until hot, 375°F on a deep-fry thermometer. Working in batches, without crowding the pot, add some of the balls to the hot oil. Fry the dough for about 2 to 3 minutes, turning it gently until golden brown. Transfer the dough, using a slotted spoon, to paper towel-lined baking sheets or platters to drain and cool. Continue in this manner until all of the dough is fried. Make sure to maintain the oil temperature before adding the next batch.

Combine the honey, anisette, tangerine or orange juice, and the sliced rind in another 6-quart pot. Place over medium heat and bring to a boil. Addall of the dough balls in manageable amounts, bathing them in the honey mixture. When all are well coated, scoop out, drain, and pile onto a favorite platter in the shape of a mound. When cooled, top with rainbow colored nonpareil and shaved almonds.

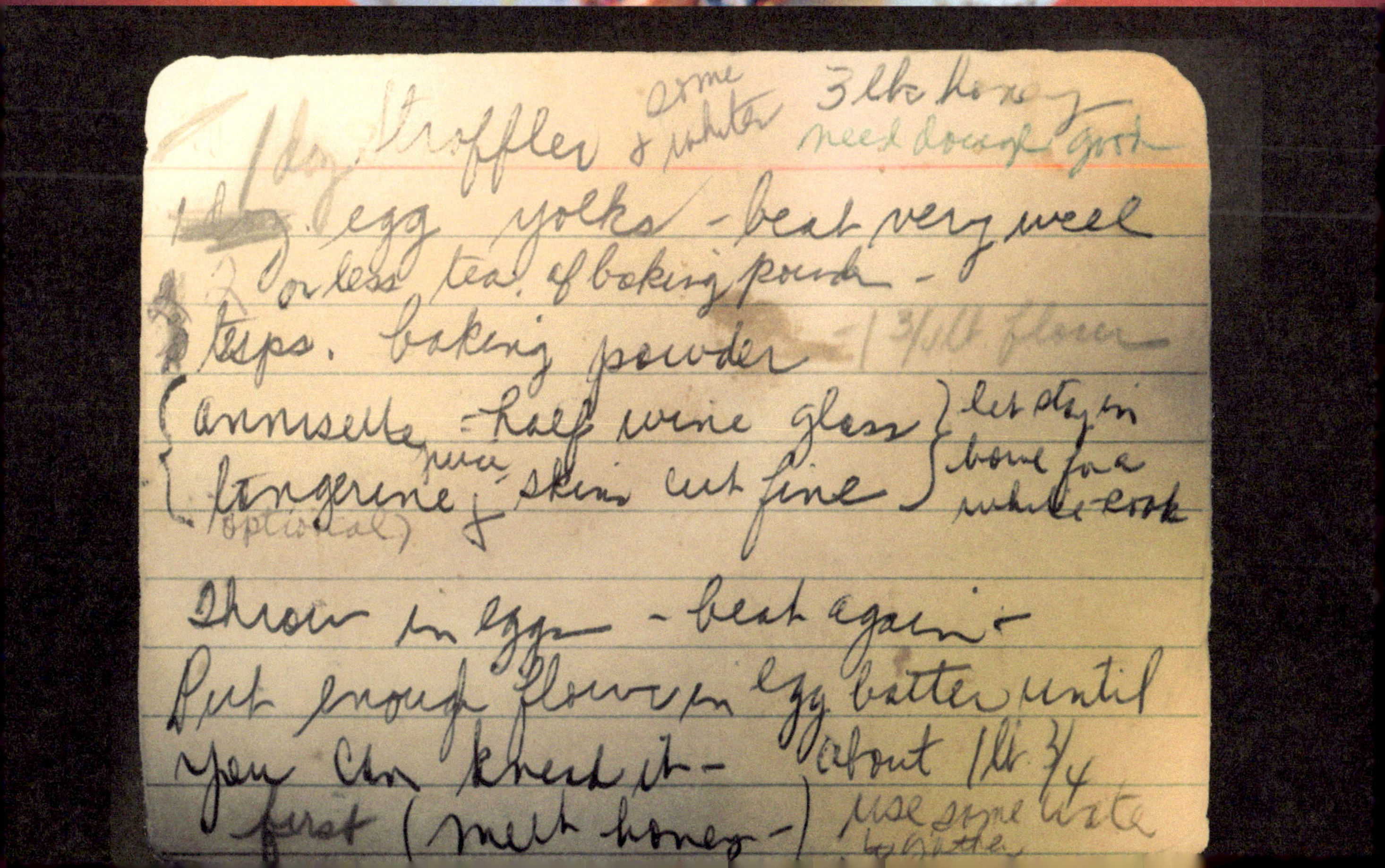

Stroffler

some white ½ — 3 lbs honey — need doesn't good

- 1 doz. egg yolks — beat very well
- 2 or less tea. of baking powder
- tsps. baking powder — 1 ¾ lb. flower
- (annisette — half wine glass) } let stay in
- (tangerine — skins cut fine)   } bowl for a
  (optional) nuts   } while — cook

Throw in eggs — beat again —
Put enough flower in egg batter until
you can knead it — about 1 lb ¾
first (melt honey —) use some water
to gather

Easter
Good Friday until Easter Sunday

Fried pizza
Mushrooms and sausage
Roasted peppers
Lamb soup
Roasted asparagus
Roasted lamb
Easter bread
Savory pie
Grain pie

Opposite: Homage to grandma Lilly who remains a spiritual advisor every Easter season. This page: Holy Week luminary on 65th Street, Brooklyn.

Aunt Jo and Uncle Joe rented the upstairs apartment after our grandmother died, and they became the new standard bearers. Tradition would now became the responsibility of the next generation. Among the many cousins of that generation, I demonstrated an early interest in cooking. Aunt Jo and Uncle Joe were more than happy to nurture my interest in making bread. It was time to be a part of our Easter culinary tradition and lasting institution.

On the Thursday night before Easter, my aunt and uncle would visit my mother's kitchen and guide me through the process of making bread, as my parents proudly watched over.

As I battled with pounds of unwieldy dough, I listened to their stories. Kneading the dough to the correct consistency took close to an hour. It was back-breaking work but the whole experience felt like a rite of passage. I didn't fully realize at that time that I was being given agency that would last a lifetime.

Above: On the 18th Avenue rooftop, from left to right, Aunt Jo; Uncle Joe; Uncle Eddie; my father, James Jr.; his mother, Lilly; and the man who gave us the magic bread-mixing bowl, my grandfather, James Sr. Below, left to right: My grandmother Louisella with Aunt Jo; Mom nervously serving her first Thanksgiving dinner in 1951; Aunt Jo in the kitchen of her tiny apartment at 44th Street, holding cousin Lilly Ann

My paternal grandfather, James Sr., ran a metal shop with his four sons in Williamsburg, Brooklyn. They made schoolhouse lighting fixtures and shades. When his wife Livia (Lilly) asked for a bowl big enough to make large quantities of Easter bread, he simply inverted one of those light fixture housings, attached two handles, glazed it, and brought it home.

Aunt Jo and Uncle Joe inherited this precious heirloom and would later hand it down to my mother and father. It was simply too big for their tiny four-room apartment in Borough Park.

Top: The bowl my grandfather made using a schoolhouse lighting fixture.
Above: Grandma Louisella and me, Valley View Dairy Farm, 1959.

Good Friday

When I was a young boy, I couldn't wait for the apparition of the colossal, speckled porcelain bowl that hung in the basement pantry. It hung on a hook, attached to a piece of string that undoubtedly came from my grandmother's clothes line. It rested against the makeshift wooden wall enveloped in a plastic shroud. Somehow, this bowl was not like any other. I always felt that its fired enamel concavity held our family history.

Each year in the run-up to Easter, the bowl would be carried with great care and ceremony into the kitchen of my grandmother's apartment, in preparation of the miracle soon to follow: The rising of the bread dough. Having mixed and kneaded the dough, the bowl would then be ceremoniously transferred to our bedroom, the warmest room of the house, where, the dough would miraculously double in size overnight.

Above: Good Friday procession of the deposed Christ along 65th Street

Pizze Fritte

Fried pizza occupies a big place in our hall of fame. As I remember it, fried pizza was introduced to me during the Lenten season: 40 days of abstaining from eating meat on the Wednesdays and Fridays before Easter. These delectable delicacies later became an occasional superstar Friday-night staple—an endlessly popular dinner option to delight and surprise children of any age. It's a Good Friday favorite that is good any day of the year. Serves 8 to 10.

Sauce:
1 tablespoon extra virgin olive oil
3 garlic cloves peeled and crushed
1 teaspoon dry Italian oregano
1½ cups drained canned plum tomatoes, crushed by hand or through a food mill or blender
1 teaspoon kosher salt
Freshly ground black pepper

Don Pepino All-Natural Pizza Sauce is a good alternative if you are pressed for time.

Heat the olive oil in a 2-quart pot, over medium-low heat. Add the garlic and sauté until it turns a rich golden color on both sides. Add oregano and crushed tomatoes while being careful the oil does not splatter. Add salt and fresh black pepper to taste. Cook at a simmer uncovered for 30 minutes. Keep warm and set aside to serve with the pizza.

Dough:
1 packet active dry yeast
1 cup warm water
1 teaspoon sugar
1 tablespoon extra virgin olive oil, plus more for the bowl to drizzle
3½ cups all-purpose flour, plus more as needed
1 teaspoon kosher salt
3 tablespoons olive oil

Combine the yeast, sugar, warm water (just warm to the touch) in a large bowl. Whisk to mix and let sit about 3 minutes until bubbly.

Coat the bowl of a standing mixer with olive oil. Arm the mixer with a dough hook, then place 2 cups of flour and the salt in the bowl. Pour in the yeast mixture and mix at medium speed about 1 to 2 minutes until a rough, sticky ball of dough comes together, adding a little more flour or water as necessary. Let the dough rest for 5 minutes in the mixer. Then mix on low about 1 minute until the dough is no longer sticky.

Oil your hands, transfer the dough to a lightly floured board or the kitchen counter, and knead about 30 seconds until very smooth. Transfer the dough to an oiled bowl and cover the surface of the bowl with plastic wrap. Refrigerate for at least 1 hour or overnight. When the dough has doubled in size remove it from the refrigerator and bring to room temperature. (A less labor-intensive alternative to the above would be to buy some pizza dough from your corner pizzeria.)

Toppings (maintain at room temperature):
1 pound of fresh mozzarella cheese, cut into small, thin slices
½ cup grated Romano cheese
2 tablespoons dry Italian oregano and ½ cup torn fresh basil

Working on a lightly floured board or the kitchen counter, pinch off enough dough to make a 4-inch-round mini pizza. Place it on the floured baking sheet. Continue in this manner until all of the dough has been used. Set the mini pizza crusts aside to rise for at least 30 minutes.

Add canola oil with a drop of extra virgin olive oil to a 10-inch skillet, over medium heat. When the oil reaches 350°F on a deep-fry thermometer, add two to three pizzas to the oil. They cook veryquickly. Fry for approximately 2 minutes, or until they are puffed and golden.

At this point, turn the pizzas over and very carefully top each one with a slice of mozzarella. The moisture in the cheese will cause the oil to splatter so best if you keep it from slipping off the crust. Remove the pizzas from the oil when the bottoms are brown and place them on a platter. Add sauce, grated cheese, oregano, and basil, if using, and a drizzle of extra virgin olive oil. Serve.

Above: My culinary consultants, Luca and Madeline, on Saturday morning, poking holes in the Easter bread dough to deflate it.

On Saturday morning, as the braided dough rose before baking, we had time to prepare the sausage pie (casatiello).

Pane di Pasqua

Easter bread that is well worth dedicating half a day to. Yields 7 to 8 loaves.

Dough:
5 packages of dry yeast (11¼ teaspoons proof yeast in a 4-cup container)
5 pounds unbleached all-purpose flour (approximately 17 cups)
1 additional pound flour for adding to dough if needed, cleaning hands, and dusting board and pans
3½ cups sugar
Pinch of salt
1 pound salted butter, softened, plus a bit more for coating rising dough
24 medium to large eggs, beaten
2 tablespoons anisette extract

Decorating:
6 ounces rainbow-colored nonpareil
3 egg yolks
3 tablespoons water

Combine the flour, sugar, and salt in a 16-quart pot. Add the butter and mix by hand, squeezing and merging butter with the flour mixture. Add proofed yeast to the flour mixture; continue mixing ingredients.

Slowly stir in all of the beaten eggs and anisette using a fork. Continue to mix until ingredients are combined and loose until dough begins to form.

Knead the dough with floured hands for approximately 45 minutes, or until it becomes smooth and elastic. Add flour to the dough if needed, or to scrape the dough off your hands and the bottom of the pot.

Once the dough is fully kneaded, leave it in the pot, lightly spread some butter over the top to keep it moist, and cover with a cloth. Leave at room temperature to rise for 8 hours or overnight. The dough is ready when it rises about 5 times its size.

When the dough has fully risen, punch it down, turn it out onto a floured surface, and form it into a ball. Cut the dough into 7 or 8 smaller dough balls using a sharp knife. Then cut each ball in half. Roll each half into strands approximately 16-inches long. To form a loaf, lay the strands side by side and cross them over at one end, offset by 3 inches.

Continue crossing one strand over the other while working the braid into a circle. The tie off can be challenging. Join the circle by tucking one end under the other, pinch the dough firmly together to seal, maintaining the twist and thickness of the loaf. Repeat with the remaining dough.

Butter and flour one 9-inch baking pan for each loaf. Place the braided loaves in individual pans and set aside, covered in a warm, draft-free place to rise for another hour until the dough rises about 30 percent more.

At this point, preheat the oven to 250°F.

When the dough has risen, place the pans into the oven for about 10 minutes, then raise the temperature to 325°F. Bake until the bread is a dark golden brown and makes a hollow sound when lightly tapped on the bottom.

Prepare the egg wash for decorating. In a small bowl, beat the 3 egg yolks with 3 tablespoons of water and set aside.

When the breads are fully baked, remove them from the oven and pan using oven mitts then decorate immediately. Brush the egg wash onto the hot surface of each loaf and sprinkle with the colored confetti. Set the loaves to cool on racks. Slice a wedge and spread with butter.

Above: Luca and Madeline showing off the sausage pie they helped create.

Our sausage pie, or casatiello, is a hybrid of a meat pie and panino, fortified with eggs, ricotta, mozzarella, Romano cheese, and finely sliced Faicco's dry fennel sausage. The final product is a thing of majesty. Its domed grandeur is an architectural wonder, somehow reminiscent of the Pantheon in Rome.

The genre of savory pies originated in and around the region of Naples and was traditionally served as a complete first meal to celebrate the end of Lent, the 40-day religious fast. My uncles could not wait until the pie completed its two-hour oven firing. What a way to break the fast.

Casatiello

Savory sausage pie alla Paterna is best served slightly warm or at room temperature, accompanied by a cold glass of Italian beer. Serves 10 to 12.

Crust:
- 4 cups all-purpose flour
- 1 teaspoon baking powder
- ½ cup vegetable shortening
- 4 medium eggs
- ½ cup ice cold water
- 1 cup whole milk for a milk wash
- 1 teaspoon freshly ground black pepper

Combine the flour, baking powder, and vegetable shortening in a large bowl or on a cutting board. Make a well and add the eggs into the center of the flour mixture. Beat the eggs with a fork while gradually taking in the dry ingredients. Mix until all of the flour is absorbed by the egg and the mixture becomes dry. Add some of the cold water, 1 tablespoon at a time, until it forms a dough. Gather into a ball, wrap in plastic, and place in the refrigerator for 30 minutes.

Filling:
- 12 medium eggs
- 2 pounds ricotta cheese, drained
- ½ pound mozzarella cheese or toma cheese
- 1¼ pound hot semi-dry sausage or your choice of cured meat, casing removed, sliced thin
- ½ cup grated Romano cheese

Lightly beat the eggs in a large bowl. Add the ricotta or toma cheese, sausage, Romano, and black pepper to the eggs. Mix well until thoroughly combined and set aside.

At this point preheat an oven to 325°F.

Spread some vegetable shortening followed by a dusting of flour in a 9-inch springform baking pan and set aside.

Remove the dough from the refrigerator and turn it out onto a lightly floured surface. Pinch off approximately ½ of the dough, cover it with the plastic, and set aside for the top crust.

Roll the remaining dough into a 15-16-inch circle. Ease it into the pan, leaving about 1½ inches of excess around the top edge. Fill the crust with the egg, cheese, and sausage mixture, and set aside.

Roll a 10-11-inch circle using the dough previously set aside for the top crust. Place it on top of the filling, pressing the pastry edges together. Curl the overlapping edges towards the center to make a tight seal. Pierce the top crust in several places using a pointy fork or the point of a sharp knife to prevent the pastry from cracking during baking.

Apply a light coating of milk over the top of the pie using a pastry brush. Place the pan in the preheated oven and bake for 2 hours until the crust is golden brown. Brush the pie every 20 to 30 minutes with the milk wash to ensure a nice golden glaze. Serve at room temperature.

Easter Sunday

As tradition would have it, we could not eat the Easter loaf until Easter morning. It was almost as exciting as Christmas Day. When I first heard our daughter ask, "Why do we give so much away?" I remembered asking the very same question of my mother. It tasted too good to give away. Generosity is also a learned custom. These offered loaves, sent to out-of-state relatives and friends, both reflect and perpetuate a tradition that inevitably binds us to one another and to our shared history.

As the leg of lamb marinates and the zuppa di agnello simmers, we complete the Easter bread ritual by packaging it in colored cellophane and bright red ribbon, ready to distribute to friends and family.

Funghi e Salsiccia Secca

Sautéed mushrooms and dried sausage—Luca's favorite. Serves 6.

2 tablespoons extra virgin olive oil
2 cloves garlic crushed
1 cup hot dried sausage, casing removed*, sliced and quartered
3 12-ounce packages of white mushrooms, cleaned and sliced
1 tablespoon dried oregano
1 teaspoon sea salt

Heat the olive oil in a 2-quart skillet over medium heat. Add the garlic and cook until it begins to brown. Add the sausage and sauté until the oil takes on a red hue and the sausage is browned.

Add the mushrooms and sauté until all their liquid evaporates and the mushrooms turn brown. Fold in the oregano and salt.

Serve at room temperature.

*To remove sausage casing, set the whole piece upright in a 1-quart container of warm water. Score the casing with a sharp knife when it turns milky white and peel it back to expose the amount of sausage you need.

Peperoni con Pinoli e Capperi

There's nothing like the fragrance of roasted peppers, pine nuts, and capers. Serves 6 to 8.

4 tablespoons
3 cloves garlic, crushed
2 tablespoons salt-cured capers
5-6 medium-sized sweet red bell peppers, sliced
2 tablespoons extra virgin olive oil
2 tablespoons pine nuts
Freshly ground black pepper
Fresh parsley, chopped

Preheat the oven to 400°F.

Combine the olive oil, garlic, capers, and peppers in a 9-by-14-inch casserole dish. Place the dish in the preheated oven. Roast for around 40 minutes until the peppers are just tender when pierced with a fork, stirring occasionally to ensure everything cooks evenly.

When the peppers reach that point, fold in the pine nuts and continue roasting for another 15 to 20 minutes or until the peppers are very tender.

Remove the dish from the oven and fold in the black pepper and parsley. Serve at room temperature.

Joe and Rocco of United Meat Market, Windsor Terrace, our purveyors of Easter meats.

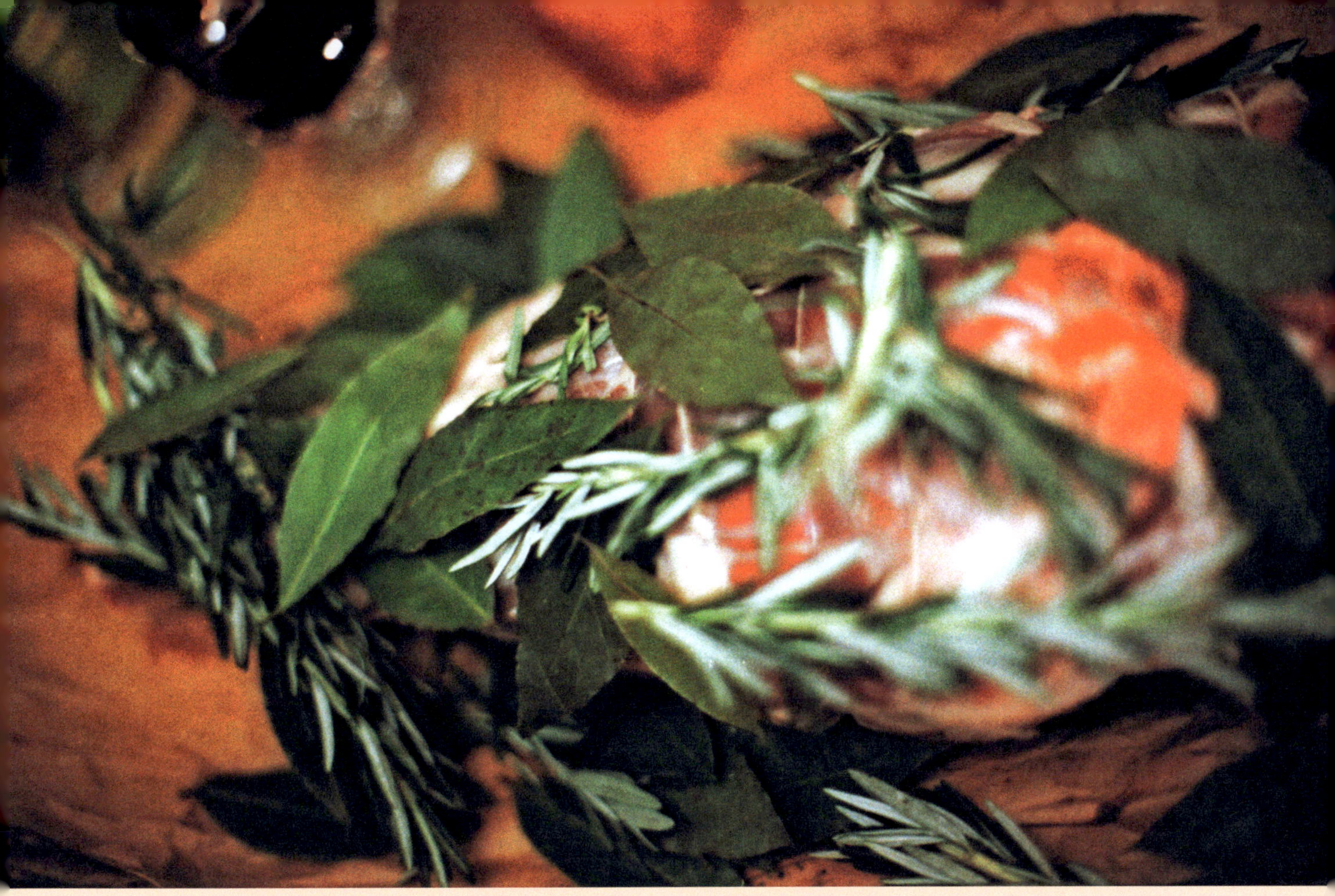

I have complete confidence in my friends at United Meat Market in Windsor Terrace, Brooklyn. Year in and year out, they deliver the sweetest, most tender lamb.

3 Lamb shanks (soup veg little)
cut 1" size
little 4 cups water olive oil put
Boil lamb in some water
celery + 2 onions. Carrots 5
when that's cooked add boiled
chickory to it (squeeze water out
of chickory + cut it into small pieces
with scissors. Then ready to
eat scramble 3 eggs add cheese

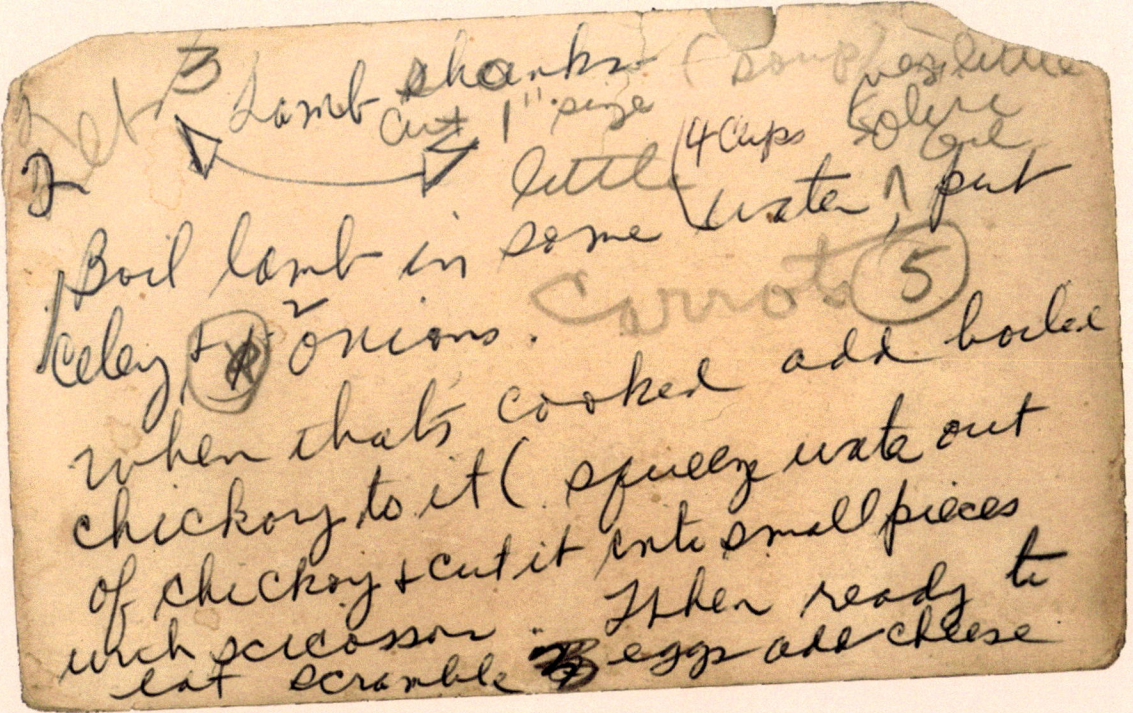

Recipe card for grandma Louisella's lamb soup

Zuppa di Agnello
Lamb shank soup alla Pastore. Serves 8.

Broth:
2 tablespoons olive oil
2 pounds lamb shanks cut into 1½-inch pieces (ask your butcher)
2½ quarts water or vegetable stock, divided (plus more to thin if necessary)
1 small carrot
½ medium onion, peeled
1 small celery stalk
1 tablespoons whole black peppercorns

Heat the oil in a 4-quart soup pot over medium-high heat. Add the lamb and lightly brown the pieces on all sides. Add 1 quart of water, the carrot, onion, celery, and peppercorns. Bring to a boil and simmer uncovered for about 1 hour. Remove the lamb and set aside.

Pour the rest of the contents into another pot or large bowl through a strainer to separate the broth. Add the remaining 1½ quarts of water (or vegetable stock) to the clear broth and set aside.

Soup:
2 tablespoons olive oil
2 onions, chopped
5 carrots, peeled and sliced
2 bunches chicory or dandelion greens, chopped
3 eggs, beaten
1 cup pecorino Romano cheese
Sea salt and freshly ground black pepper to taste
1/4 cup fresh parsley, chopped

Heat the olive oil in the original pot over medium heat. Add the chopped onions and sauté until they become translucent. Return the lamb to the pot along with the broth and bring to a boil. Reduce heat to a simmer and continue cooking for 30 minutes. Add the sliced carrots and chicory or dandelion greens. Continue to simmer until the lamb is tender and just about pulling from the bone.

Beat the eggs, Romano cheese, pepper, and parsley in a separate bowl. Set aside and leave at room temperature.

Bring the soup to a rolling boil just before serving. Slowly add the egg mixture so it forms a solid. Gently break up the egg using a fork to disperse it around the soup.

To serve, ladle the soup into bowls with some of the very tender lamb. Add salt to taste.

Lamb is most tender in the spring. Its mild flavor, in combination with the earthiness of cousin Viola's asparagus, embodies the essence of spring.

Agnello Arrosto con Asparagi Arrosto

Roasted lamb with roasted asparagus. Serves 8-10.

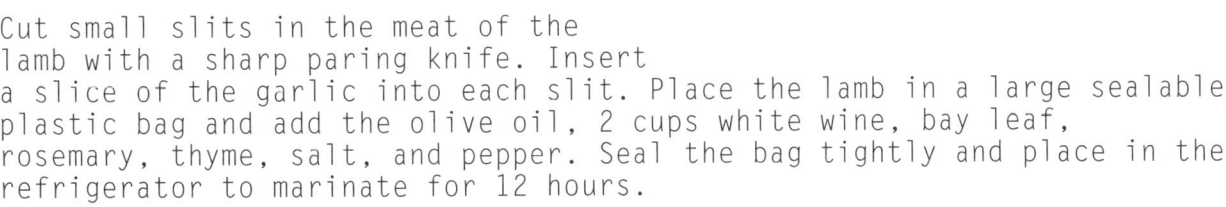

Lamb:
1 leg of lamb or loin of lamb, about 4-5 pounds
5 garlic cloves, sliced
2 tablespoons olive oil
4 cups dry white wine
1 fresh bay leaf
4 sprigs fresh rosemary
4-5 sprigs of fresh thyme

Cut small slits in the meat of the lamb with a sharp paring knife. Insert a slice of the garlic into each slit. Place the lamb in a large sealable plastic bag and add the olive oil, 2 cups white wine, bay leaf, rosemary, thyme, salt, and pepper. Seal the bag tightly and place in the refrigerator to marinate for 12 hours.

Remove the lamb from the fridge the next day, at least 4 hours before roasting. Keep the lamb sealed in the marinade bag and allow it to come to room temperature.

Heat the oven to 400°F. Remove the lamb from the bag with marinade. Place it on a rack in a roasting pan. Add 2 cups of wine. Roast for 1½ hours or until the thermometer reads 150-160°F. Baste with drippings while roasting. Serve warm.

Asparagus:
4 pounds of asparagus, remove woody ends
2 cups coarse bread crumbs
1 cup grated Romano cheese
2 tablespoons garlic powder
Freshly ground black pepper to taste
4 large eggs
Sea salt to taste

Preheat the oven to 400°F.

Place the bread crumbs, cheese, garlic powder, and black pepper in a dish or bowl wide enough to hold the asparagus. Mix well to combine thoroughly.

Put the eggs in another dish or bowl of similar size and beat well. Working in batches, dip the spears into the egg, making sure they are coated well. Immediately place them in the bread crumb mixture and toss until each spear is fully coated. Transfer the breaded asparagus to a large baking sheet.

Place the asparagus in the preheated oven and bake for 30 minutes or until the breading is browned and crispy. Serve with wedges of fresh lemon.

Easter Pie

Easter pie is a close cousin of the torta dolce di ricotta (see page 156). The recipe for the Easter pie expands that of the ricotta pie, with the addition of wheat berries, custard, and thousand flower essence. It is said the introduction of whole grain to this recipe began after grain was shipped to Italy during a famine. Italians added uncooked grain directly into the pie, instead of waiting for it to be ground down to make bread. I can't attest to the veracity of the story, but the addition of wheat berry is certainly a stroke of culinary genius. I swear there are guests who join us simply because they want to commune with this pie.

Above: Cooked skinless wheat berry along with citrus rind

Opposite page, top: My mother ready to apply confectioner's sugar to her famous pastiera napoletana. Is it a dessert or meal in its own right? The debate continues—I often enjoy it as breakfast.
Opposite page, bottom: Ricotta, sugar, egg, custard, and barley filling

La Pastiera Napoletana di Grano

Grain pie or Easter pie is made with grain, usually cooked the day before it is served. Each pie serves 8.

Crust:
2 cups all-purpose flour, plus extra to dust board and pan
¾ cup sugar
½ cup unsalted butter, softened, plus extra to grease the pan
2 medium eggs unrefrigerated

Place the flour, sugar, and zest on a pastry board or clean, dry flat surface. Mix thoroughly to combine. Add the butter and work it into the dry ingredients. Gather the mixture into a mound and create a well in the center.

Place the eggs into the center of the well. Beat the eggs with a fork, gradually incorporating the flour mixture into the eggs. When all of the dry ingredients are absorbed by the egg mixture, gather the dough with your hands and knead it into a ball. Wrap the dough in plastic wrap and refrigerate for 1 hour.

Butter and flour two 9-inch baking pans. Set aside.

Meanwhile, prepare the filling, starting with the custard.

Custard:
½ cup sugar
5 teaspoons flour
2 cups whole milk
1 teaspoon vanilla
1 peeled lemon rind
4 medium egg yolks

Combine the sugar, milk, vanilla, flour, and eggs in a small saucepan. Cook over medium heat, stirring often until the mixture becomes like pudding. Remove it from the heat and allow to cool.

Filling:
8 medium eggs
1 pound cooked pearl barley (can also use Fratelli D'Amico brand)
3 pounds ricotta cheese, drained
2 teaspoons vanilla
1½ cups sugar
2 teaspoon Aroma Millefiori (a thousand flowers) concentrate, optional
¼ cup candied pear, optional

Using a fork, combine the eggs, barley, cheese, vanilla, sugar, and Aroma Millefiori in a large bowl. Mix thoroughly, do not use a mixer. Fold the cooled custard into the filling mixture and set aside while you prepare the crust. If you can't find pre-boiled barley, make your own by boiling barley for approximately 30 minutes in a medium saucepan with the rind of one orange.

Remove the dough from the refrigerator and place it on a lightly floured surface. Pinch off ¼ of the dough, cover it with the plastic, and set aside for the lattice/crosshatch* top crust. Roll the larger piece out into a 14-15-inch circle. Now roll the dough over the rolling pin and carefully unwind it over the springform baking pan, gently easing it to fit evenly in the bottom and up the sides of the pan. Pour or spoon the filling mixture into the crust, leaving about 1 inch below the rim of the pan.

Heat the oven to 350°F.

Roll a circle out of the smaller piece of dough previously set aside for the top crust. Cut the circle into 1-inch strips. Place the strips in a lattice/crosshatch* pattern across the top of the pie filling. Place it in the preheated oven and bake for 1 hour and 45 minutes or until middle is slightly firm and top is golden.

Cool for at least 2 hours. I have left it unrefrigerated overnight to save time.

Carefully run a plastic knife or ridged spatula between crust and side of the pan to remove it, so no crust is pulled away when you release the spring of the pan. Serve at room temperature with a dusting of confectioner's sugar.

*I use four strips for each pie, but a lattice of 6 strips is more traditional, if you have enough dough left over.

Daily Dishes

Every nightime meal I shared with my family felt like a special occasion. Each dish, from the the humble to the highly elaborate, represented a labor of love. It was a symbol of the connection that brought us together as a family. From a simple bowl of pasta e fagioli to stuffed calimari, each dish still speaks of my childhood home. Each dish has its own story.

Thursday night was Mom's late-night shift at work. As I entered my teens, my mother took on full-time employment at what was then South Brooklyn Savings Bank. It was there that she met a young Michael Lomonaco, who would later attain celebrity chef status. Because of lingering gender norms, she still cooked our dinner, which my dad would reheat. Meatball stew was one of the Thursday night meals, Many decades later, this stew still reminds me of the pride my mother took in her job and in the contribution she made to our two-paycheck family.

```
        MEATBALL STEW      2lbs     ONION & GARLIC
                        chop meat      (1) can tomato
     MAKE MEATBALL  SAME  WAY EXCEPT DON'T ADD RAISENS &
     BITE SIZE.    USE (1) BAG CARROTS   ...POTATOES
     ---------------------------------------------------
         PREPARING MEATBALLS (REGULAR SIZE)   USING SLICE BREAD
         2 LBS CHOP MEAT  USE    SLICES WHITE BREAD
         DOLORES MAKES HER MEATBALLS...1 lb. chop meat -
              cup water ..add water gradually
         MEATBALLS WITH STALE ITALIAN BREAD.
         2LBS. CHOP MEAT &     OZS. of SOAKED SQUEEZED BREAD)
         TOTAL WEIGHT   SHOULD BE 3 lbs. when bread is added.
         USE   OZS. OF (stale Italian wet bread) for
         2 LBS. OF CHOP MEAT
```

Spezzatino di Polpette
Meatball stew can be prepared the night before. Serves 6.

1½ pounds meatball mixture (page 178, omit the raisins)
3 tablespoons olive oil
6-7 Yukon Gold potatoes, peeled and quartered
3 cloves garlic, chopped
2 medium sweet onions, chopped
1 28-ounce can of plum tomatoes, crushed by hand or quick blend
4 cups frozen peas
1 teaspoon sea salt, divided, more or less to taste
1 teaspoon freshly ground black pepper, divided

Roll 2-inch meatballs according to the recipe, omitting the raisins.

Heat the olive oil in a 6-quart pot over medium heat. Add the meatballs when the oil is hot, and fry until they are browned on all sides. Remove them from the pot with a slotted spoon and set aside.

Add the potatoes to the same pot and brown on all sides. Remove from heat and set aside.

Still using the same pot, add the garlic and onions and sauté until just golden brown. Season with 1 teaspoon of salt and 1 teaspoon of pepper. Add the tomatoes and potatoes. Bring to a boil, then reduce heat to a simmer. Add the meatballs and peas and simmer uncovered for 45 minutes to 1 hour or until it thickens.

Mafalda con Cavolfiore
Aunt Jo's cauliflower and mafalda pasta recipe. Serves 4.

3 tablespoons olive oil
½ cup pine nuts
1 onion, chopped
1 tablespoon sea salt, divided, more or less to your taste
1 teaspoon red chili pepper flakes, more or less to your taste, optional
2 28-ounce cans plum tomatoes, blended for 5 seconds
¼ cup dried black raisins or currents
1 head cauliflower, cut into florets, or 2 10-ounce boxes frozen
½ pound mafalda dry pasta
½ teaspoon grated pecorino Romano cheese for topping, optional

Sauté the pine nuts until light toasted. Remove from the pot and set aside. Add the onion to the pot and sauté until translucent. Add ½ teaspoon of salt and chili flakes (if using) and sauté for 30 seconds or until the oil has a red hue around the flakes. Do not burn.

Stir in the tomatoes and raisins, then cover the pot and bring to a boil over medium heat. Add the florets, reduce the heat to low, cover the pot, and simmer 45 minutes or until the cauliflower is tender. Season to taste.

Bring a large pot of water to a boil. Add salt, then pasta, and bring back to a boil. Cook until the pasta is al dente. Strain the pasta, saving a cup of pasta water. Place the pasta back in the pot, fold in some sauce adding pasta water if needed. Top with additional sauce when serving.

Pasta con Lenticchie

Pasta with lentils is a major staple in our family. The lentils can be served as a soup one night and paired with half-sized spaghetti on another night. It's a key recipe for parents on the go. Serves 4.

3-4 tablespoons olive oil
2 cloves garlic, chopped
1 medium sweet onion, chopped
1 carrot, peeled and chopped
1 celery stalk, chopped
8 ounces dry brown lentils, rinsed
3-4 cups chicken or vegetable stock
2 sprigs fresh rosemary
Sea salt and freshly ground black pepper to taste
8 ounces spaghetti, broken in half

Heat the olive oil in a 4-quart pot over medium heat. Add rosemary to flavor the oil for 4 minutes. Remove but reserve the rosemary. Add garlic followed by onions. Sauté about 4 minutes until the onions become translucent. Add the carrots and celery and continue sautéing for 2 minutes. Stir in the lentils and broth and bring everything to a boil. Cover, reduce the heat, and simmer for 60 minutes or until the lentils are tender but not falling apart. Add the rosemary for the last 10 minutes of cooking.

Bring a large pot of water to a full boil. Add salt and spaghetti and cook until the pasta is al dente. Strain the pasta, saving a cup of pasta water. Place the pasta back in the pot. Remove the rosemary from the lentils. Fold the lentils into the spaghetti, adding some pasta water if you prefer a soupier dish. Season to taste with salt and black pepper. Top with grated cheese and crushed red pepper if desired.

Pasta con Fagioli

Pasta with beans—the brick and mortar of my culinary life. Serves 4.

4 tablespoons extra virgin olive oil
4 cloves garlic, minced
1 stalk celery, sliced
32 ounces canned white or red cannellini beans, drained
1 cup vegetable or chicken broth
1 tablespoon sea salt, divided
8 ounces ditalini pasta
Freshly ground black pepper to taste
1 tablespoon grated pecorino Romano cheese for topping
Red chili pepper flakes, optional

Heat the olive oil in a 2-quart pot over medium-low heat. Add the garlic and sauté just until it begins to turn golden. Add the celery and sauté for another minute.

Add the beans and broth and bring to a boil. Reduce the heat to low and simmer for 30 minutes. Season to taste with salt and pepper.

Bring a large pot of water to a boil. Add salt and pasta, bring back to a boil and cook until the pasta is al dente. Strain the pasta, saving a cup of pasta water. Place the pasta back in the pot, fold in, adding some of the pasta water to make a slightly soup-like consistency.

Serve topped with grated cheese and chili pepper flakes.

Lardarielli

Grandma's stewed flat beans recipe inspired us to eat more vegetables. Serves 4.

1 pound fresh flat or string beans, trimmed
1 tablespoon salt, divided, more or less to your taste
4 tablespoons extra virgin olive oil
Freshly ground black pepper to taste
1 cup tomato sauce (page 167)
2 cloves garlic, cracked
1 tablespoon dry Italian oregano

Heat the olive oil in a large skillet over low heat. Add the garlic and sauté until a nice dark brown. Add the tomato sauce, salt, and pepper to taste to the pan and simmer for 20 minutes. Remove the pan from the heat.

Add the oregano then add the dtring beans to the pan and fold, coating all string beans with tomato sauce. Cover and simmer on low for at least 45 minutes or until the beans are soft and the seam looks just about ready to split open.

Serve on a platter, centering brown garlic on top.

This dish always brings back memories of Nonna Louisella.

Cotoletta e Peperoni Fritti

I describe this dish as the Southern Italian version of chicken Milanese. Serves 6.

Peppers:
2 tablespoons extra virgin olive oil
3 cloves garlic, crushed
5-6 sweet red bell peppers, sliced
1½ cups tomato sauce (page 167)
1 tablespoon sea salt, more or less to your taste
1 teaspoon freshly ground black pepper, more or less to your taste

Heat the olive oil in a 12-inch skillet over medium heat. Add the garlic and peppers. Cook for about 15-20 minutes until the peppers are tender and browned. Seeing caramelization in some areas is ideal. Fold in the tomato sauce, salt, and black pepper. Mix well and remove from the heat. Cover and set aside.

Chicken cutlets:
1½ pounds thin cut chicken cutlets
Juice from 1 fresh lemon
½ cup all-purpose flour
3-4 eggs beaten
2 cups dry Italian bread crumbs
16 ounces olive oil or canola oil
¼ cup chopped fresh parsley

Place the chicken in a medium-sized bowl, toss with the lemon juice, and set aside to marinate for about 15 minutes.

Prepare three separate shallow platters—one with the flour, another with the eggs, and the last with the bread crumbs. Dip each cutlet in that order from left to right. First into the flour, coating both sides, then into the egg to coat well, and lastly into the bread crumbs. Gently press each side of the cutlet into the crumbs using the back of a fork to ensure the egg coating sticks. Repeat the process for the rest of the cutlets.

Prepare a large baking sheet lined with paper towels or a rack. Set aside.

Heat the oil in a 9-inch skillet over medium heat to 350°F on a deep-fry thermometer. If you are not using a thermometer, the oil is hot enough for frying when you see the oil surface ripple like a mirage, and dipping in one edge of the cutlet causes a quick foaming reaction.

Working in batches, carefully place a cutlet or two into the hot oil. Fry about 2 minutes on each side until you notice a deep crispy golden brown.

Remove the cutlets from the pan and set on the prepared baking sheet to drain off any excess oil. Making sure the oil comes back up to temperature between batches, repeat for the rest of the chicken cutlets. Be careful not to stack them to prevent them from losing crispness.

To serve, place a chicken cutlet on a plate and top with juicy peppers and fresh parsley.

Pollo alla Griglia con Limone e Origano

Grilled chicken with lemon and oregano. Serves 6.

1 clove garlic, crushed
Juice of 4 large fresh lemons
1 large lemon, sliced
1 tablespoons dried Sicilian or Greek oregano, more for garnish
1½ teaspoons sea salt, divided, more or less to taste
1 teaspoon freshly ground black pepper
4 tablespoons extra virgin olive oil, plus more to coat chicken
1½ pounds chicken cutlet, cut thin if possible

Prepare the marinade. Rub the inside of a small bowl with the garlic and leave the clove in the bowl. Add the lemon juice, oregano, salt, and pepper. Whisk in the olive oil and set aside.

Place the cutlets on a flat surface and coat them with olive oil and salt. Set aside.

Heat an iron grill pan, griddle with ridges, or a charcoal grill. When the grill is very hot, grill all the cutlets about 1 to 2 minutes on each side, making sure you get a good sear on the chicken before turning.

Place the cutlets on a flat serving platter. Pour the lemon marinade over the chicken, top with sliced lemon, dust with additional oregano, and don't forget fresh bread for dipping.

Bistecca di Manzo alla Pizzaiola

Beef steak with tomatoes is a dish prepared using ingredients readily available to a pizza maker. Serves 6.

2 pounds cherry or grape tomatoes
1½ pounds skirt steak cut in 3-inch pieces, lightly salted
2 cloves randomly chopped garlic for steak
2 cloves cracked garlic for tomatoes
4 tablespoons extra virgin olive oil
1 sprig of fresh oregano, leaves only
2 branches of fresh basil, leaves only
1 tablespoon salt and black pepper to taste

Heat 2 tablespoons of the oil in a 4-quart pot over medium heat. Add two cracked garlic cloves and half of the basil. Sauté until the garlic just begins to turn golden, then add the tomatoes and salt. Cover and simmer on low for about 40 minutes until the tomatoes become soft. Remove and season to taste.

Place a skillet over medium heat and, once hot, sear each piece of steak quickly and remove to a plate. Be careful not to cook it through. Heat the remaining 2 tablespoons of oil in the same skillet used to sear the steak. Add the remaining garlic and quickly sauté for about 1 minute. Add the cooked tomatoes and stir, loosening the brown bits from the bottom of the pan. Return the steak, along with its juices, to the pan. Reduce the heat to low, cover, and simmer with the tomatoes for 5 to 10 minutes.

To serve, spoon the sauce onto a platter, place the steak on the sauce, and top with the remaining oregano, torn basil leaves, and a nice amount of black pepper. Like having built-in steak sauce.

Insalata di Peperoni e Patate

Our summertime roasted pepper and potato salad. Serves 4 to 6.

6 red bell peppers (can use jarred)
6-8 Yukon Gold potatoes
1 large clove garlic crushed
1 tablespoon sea salt, more or less to taste
1 teaspoon freshly ground black pepper, more or less to taste
5 tablespoons extra virgin olive oil, plus a drizzle for serving
4 eggs, hard-boiled, sliced in half
½ cup chopped fresh Italian parsley

Broil the peppers until the skin is black on all sides. Remove from the heat and place them in a paper bag for 20 minutes to cool and loosen the skin. When the peppers are cool enough to handle, remove the charred skin as much as you can. You can quickly rinse without removing too much flavor. Slice the peppers into 1½-inch-wide slices. Set aside.

Place the potatoes in a medium-large saucepan. Add enough water to cover them completely and boil the potatoes about 20 minutes, until they are fork tender. Remove them from the water, let cool, peel, and cut into quarters.

Rub garlic all around the inside of a large mixing bowl. Add the peppers, potatoes, salt, black pepper, and olive oil. Toss gently to combine.

To serve, spoon the potatoes and peppers onto a large flat serving platter. Arrange halved eggs over the top and sprinkle with parsley. Drizzle with additional olive oil and season to your taste.

Insalata di Zucchini con Menta Fresca
Grandma Louisella's zucchini and fresh mint salad. Serves 6.

4 medium zucchini
1 large clove garlic crushed
1 tablespoon sea salt, or to your taste
1 teaspoon freshly ground black pepper, or to your taste
1 cup apple cider vinegar or white balsamic vinegar
1/2 cup extra virgin olive oil, plus more for the grill
Fresh Italian mint leaves, torn

Trim both ends of the zucchini and cut lengthwise into ½-inch slices and brush with olive oil.

Prepare the marinade. Rub the garlic all around the inside of a serving bowl and leave the clove in the bowl. Add salt, pepper, and vinegar, and mix by swirling everything around the sides of the bowl to pick up the garlic flavor. Whisk in the olive oil using a fork. Set aside

Heat a ribbed griddle pan over medium-high heat or prepare a charcoal grill. When the griddle is hot, brush the surface of the pan or grill rack with olive oil. Sear the slices on both sides quickly so the zucchini does not overcook and become too soft.

Place all of the zucchini into the serving bowl with the prepared marinade, along with the mint, and gently fold until the slices are well coated. Let sit for 30 minutes, then gently fold again, adding more salt, pepper, vinegar, or olive oil to your tastes.

Ciambotta

My mom's vegetable stew. If I had to pick a desert-island dish, this may just be it—with a piece of crusty bread, of course. Serves 6.

3 tablespoons olive oil
6 small potatoes, peeled and quartered
2 cloves garlic crushed
2 large sweet onions, peeled and quartered
Fresh oregano leaves from 2 sprigs
Fresh basil leaves from 2 branches
5 small zucchini, sliced
4 sweet red peppers, sliced
1 pound medium-size eggplant, sliced and quartered
35 ounces canned plum tomatoes, chopped
1 tablespoon salt, more or less to taste
Freshly ground black pepper, to taste
Parmigiano cheese, dry chili flakes for topping, optional

Heat the olive oil in a 4-quart pot over medium heat. Add the potatoes and garlic and cook about 15 minutes until the potatoes are golden brown on all sides. Remove the potatoes and set aside. Add the onions to the same pot and cook until they are golden brown. Add the oregano and basil to the onions and sauté for 1 minute more.

Add the zucchini, sweet peppers, and eggplant, and sauté for another 10 minutes. Stir in the tomatoes, salt, and black pepper, cover, and bring to a boil. Reduce the heat and simmer for 1 hour. After the 1 hour of cooking, return the potatoes to the pot and continue simmering for 1 more hour. Season to taste.

Serve the stew in a bowl with grated parmigiano cheese, crushed red pepper, and some crusty bread.

Crab Fest
We celebrate Robert's birthday with an annual crab fest. The festivities start with an outing to the fish market to select the plumpest blue claw crabs.

Robert with his favorite niece and nephew

239

Granchi alla Marinara

Crabs in a marinara sauce. Serves 6 to 8.

24 female blue claw crabs, buy them alive
    (You can distinguish female crabs by their wider apron)
3 tablespoons olive oil
4 cloves garlic, chopped
2-3 tablespoons crushed red chili pepper flakes
½ cup white wine
6 28-ounce cans of plum tomatoes, slightly pureed
16 ounces tomato paste
1 teaspoon dry oregano
1 tablespoon salt
1½ pounds spaghetti or lingune

Cleaning the crabs:
Fill a container, large enough to hold the crabs, with ice and cold water. Add the live crabs and let them sit in the ice bath for 5 minutes. This will stun them and make it easier to work with them barehanded. Holding the crab by its legs (not claws), lift up one pointy end of the top shell and pry it off. This instantly kills the crab. Flip it over and remove the T-shaped apron from the underside. Remove the mouth parts and scoop out the entrails. Scrape off the spongy gills from both halves and rinse.

Heat the olive oil in an 8-10-quart saucepan over medium-low heat. Add the crabs, top face-down to cover the bottom of the pot. Sauté them until they are slightly brown or until the shell just turns red. Remove from the pot and set aside.

Add the garlic to the same oil and sauté for 1 minute. Add the crushed chili pepper and sauté for 1 minute more. Add the wine and simmer about 3 minutes until it evaporates.

Stir in the tomatoes, tomato paste, oregano, and salt. Cover and bring to a boil. Return the crabs to the pot just as the sauce begins to boil. Reduce the heat and simmer uncovered for about 2 hours so that the sauce thickens and is flavored with juice from the crabs.

Airplane Fish

As a child I was not a fan of squid, until my father had the brilliant idea of rebranding it as "airplane fish."

Squid has occupied a special place in my family's heart. I remember my grandmother laboring over two dozen stuffed calamari to bring to her doctor in appreciation for making an emergency call. I remember double parking in front of his office one rainy night while my mother escorted our now ailing Louisella. Between them, they carried a 10-quart pot fresh off of her stove. It was one of the most earnest acts of gratitude my young eyes had ever seen. The acts of kindness by my aunt and grandmother have never been forgotten.

There is a restaurant in Boston's North End named The Daily Catch that once staked their reputation on stuffed squid. Due to lack of demand, they no longer serve the dish. Luckily, we still do. They have a truly sweet, amazing taste, well worth the effort.

My mom's handwritten recipe card documents her trial-and-error approach to developing the ultimate recipe for this wonderful dish

Stuffed Squid -
get at least 6 lbs of cleaned squid get larger size
stuffing: before putting squid in sauce leave them out at room
3 eggs
plenty of grated cheese
pignoli + raisins
garlic + parsley
salt + (black pepper)

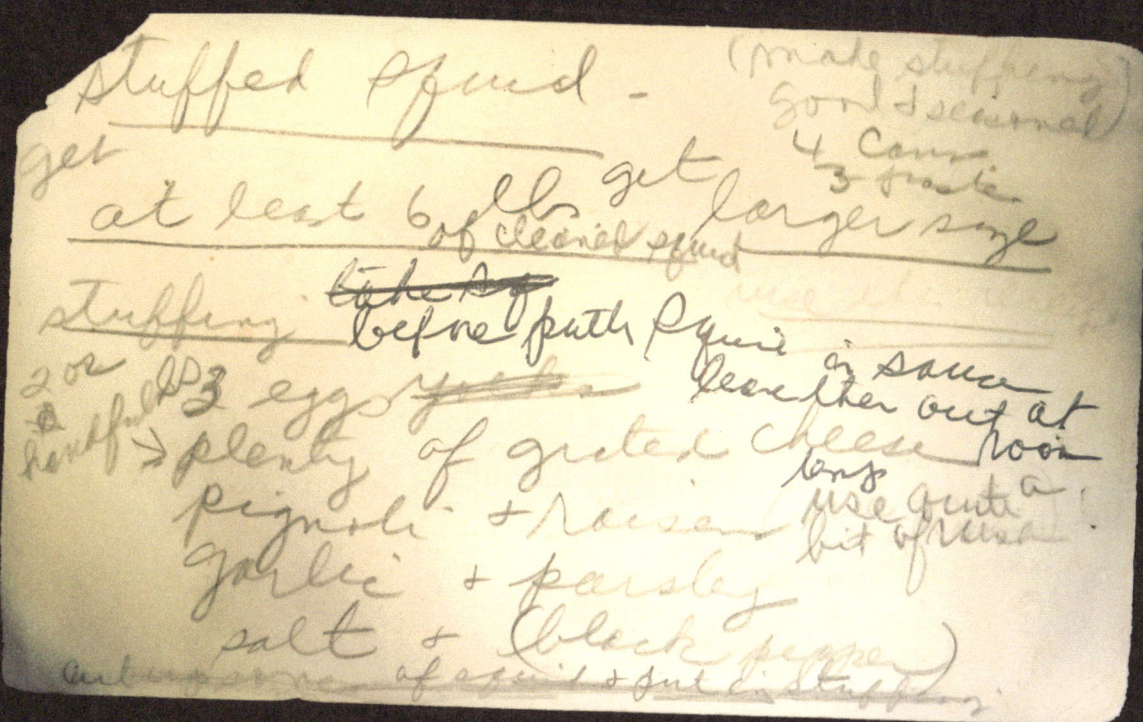

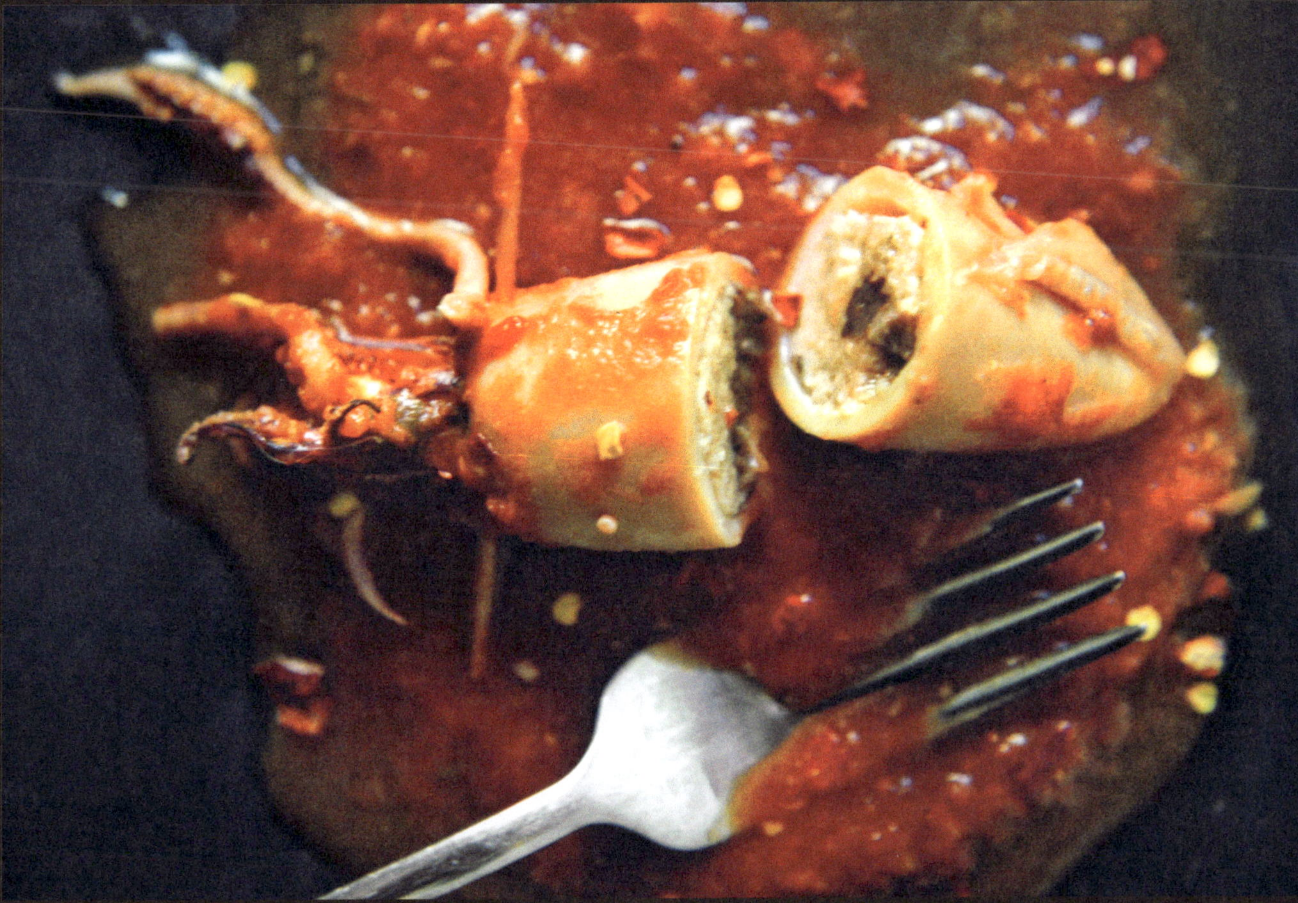

Calamari Ripieni
Stuffed squid or, in Neapolitan, calamari imbottiti. Serves 8 to 10.

5 pounds medium-sized calamari, with tentacles, cleaned and drained

Sauce:
3 tablespoons olive oil
4 cloves garlic, chopped
½ cup white wine
4 28-ounce cans of plum tomatoes, slightly puréed
16-ounce cans of tomato paste
1 tablespoon salt

Heat the oil in a large 6-quart pot over low heat. Add the garlic and sauté for 1 minute. Add the wine and simmer until the alcohol cooks off. Stir in the tomatoes, tomato paste, and salt. Raise the heat and bring to a quick boil. Reduce the heat to the lowest level and simmer slowly while you stuff the calamari.

Stuffing:
3 medium eggs
½ cup grated Romano cheese
¼ cup cup pine nuts
2 tablespoons chopped parsley
1½ cups bread crumbs
½ teaspoon freshly ground black pepper
1 teaspoon sea salt, more or less to taste
¼ cup raisins, optional

Beat the eggs in a small mixing bowl. Add the cheese, pine nuts, parsley, bread crumbs, salt, pepper, and raisins, and mix to combine thoroughly.

Using a teaspoon, fill the body of each calamari to a little more than half full. Be careful not to overstuff them as the calamari will shrink dramatically while they simmer in the sauce.

Using round toothpicks as skewers, attach the tentacles to the body through the opening. Make sure it is a snug attachment, then set aside. Apply the same process to the all of the calamari.

When all of the calamari are stuffed and the tentacles attached, gently place them into the sauce one by one. Cook in the simmering sauce for approximately 45 minutes until they are tender when pierced with a fork.

Carefully remove the toothpicks. Serve as a meal. Use the sauce on a plate of linguine, as first course, then serve stuffed calamari as a second course.

PASSING IT ON

Family, Friends, and Food
(page 248)

Anne's Legacy
(page 250)

Thank You
(page 250)

Louisa's 90-year old fork. Grandma used this fork seemingly to cook everything, before specialized cooking tools were in vogue.

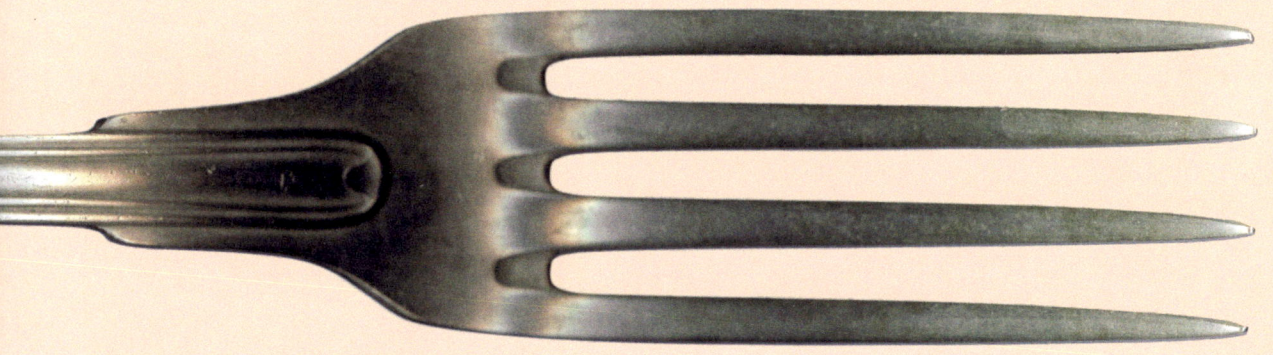

Left: My grandma Louisa in her original home in Italy 1916. Right: One of my two young assistants asking for a break in 2011.

Family, Friends, and Food

All faith-based culinary traditions form a circle around our lives, an annual progression that becomes richer with time. The batches of bread and holiday dishes disappear until they symbolically return.

The meal has been prepared, the food has been eaten, the guests have departed, yet, as the house empties, a feeling of joy and contentment persists. My hope is that the rituals and the traditions connected to these festive meals will similarly bring joy to the next generation.

What I have faithfully recreated will hopefully inspire the next generation to carry on the simple wish of our departed. That we may sit together with our loved ones to share a meal and to reinforce the bonds that bring us together is what matters most.

As if their births weren't already the greatest gifts, our children, Luca and Madeline, have patiently humored me by, posing, helping with lighting, shopping, and cooking with me while documenting these special times. May they someday know the joy of parenting too.

Traditions evolve to embrace changing times and circumstances. Over the years, we have created an extended family and a wide circle of friends of all faiths. My wife coined the phrase "J-Easter" to lessen our Jewish guests' guilt for breaking their own Passover, which often coincides with Easter. Nothing can be better than the times we have spent with all of them. It was especially satisfying for my mother to share her traditions with people of different faiths and nationalities.

Anne's legacy

Mom's recipe box returns to our kitchen table every holiday

My mother (far left), age 10, with her sisters and cousins, 61st Street, Brooklyn, October 1939. Of all the images of her, this one best captures the essence of her happiest times.

My mother, Anne, died on January 14, 2013 at the age of 84, as this book was beginning to be developed.

My mother was challenged by ill health her whole life. She contracted scarlet fever as a young girl. Its aftereffects would plague her throughout her long life.

Anne was often described as "living in the past." I suffer the same joyful affliction. In a sense, her deep connection to the past was a way of coping with her early awareness of mortality. She clung to what she referred to as "happy times." These happy times often centered around family gatherings, celebrations, and the special dishes described in this book.

Thank you

to Luca, Madeline, and Audra for your endless patience and support. Thank you to my beloved mom, Anne Paterna, my inspirational father, James Paterna, Aunt Josephine and Uncle Joe Paterna, my grandmother Louisa Pastore, and my steadfast brother, Robert Paterna.

I also want to thank the following individuals for their help and support: Daniel Power, Michael Lomonaco, John Turturro, Michael Gerbino, Rocco Amato, Simone Procas, Edward Lewine, Heather Rignanesi, Melissa Schreiber, Vicky Lemont, Dana Burnell, Rossella Rago, Francesca Marie Cwynar, Jill Novatt, Emiliano Cammardella, Monica Cammardella, Irma Schreiber, Kieran Patten, Thomas Roma and Anna Friendlander at SPQR, my therapist Leslie Zeigler, and Pietro Alongi for fortifing my voice.

Finally I have great gratitude and appreciation to all the business owners who gave freely of their time: Antonio Garritano at Little Records; Nino Mannino, Anthony Turrigiano, and George Ferrantello at Bari Pork Store; Vito Conigliaro at J & V Pizza; Alfredo Ferrara, George Switzer, and Frank Caragiulo at Queen Ann Ravioli; Joseph Generoso at Paneantico; Matt and Louie Faicco at Faicco's Pork Store; Angela and Emanuele and Angela Alaimo at Villabate; Frank and Frank, Jr. Gassoso at Frank & Sal; Mario Giura and family at Saverese; Joseph Ajello at Pastosa; Michilina and Sal Salzarulo at Lioni Latticini; Pasquale Lorina at Papa Pasquale; Rocco and Joe Gallo at United Meat Market; Louie and Dominic Coluccio at Coluccio's; Louis Coluccio, Jr. at A.L.C. Alimentary; and finally Angelo, Joseph, and Lilly Bono at Sea Breeze II.

My mother waiting in line at Sea Breeze II, many Christmases ago. She is holding her shopping list and a pen in her hands. There is something about this image that ties together so many thoughts and emotions. I firmly belicve that the progression of this book over eight years was guided by her spirit.

Index of Recipes

Chicken
Chicken Cutlet with Fried Peppers 230
Ciambotta 236
Grilled Chicken with Lemon and Oregano 232

Desserts
Easter Bread 204
Grain Pie (Pastiera) 222
Lemon Drops 82
Ricotta Sweet Pie 156
"S" Cookies 67
Struffoli 192
Saint Joseph Pastry
 (Zeppole di San Giuseppe) 50

Fish
Air-dried Cod (Stoccafisso) 140
Baked Shrimp 150
Crabs Frà Diavolo 240
Dried Codfish (Baccalà) Salad 134
Fried Fish Platter 143
Marinated Eel with Mint 151
Octopus Sauce 143
Seafood Salad 136
Scungilli 153
Shrimp Marinara 121
Stuffed Calamari 244

Fried Pizza 200

Lamb
Lamb Shank Soup 216
Roasted Lamb 219

Meat
Braciola 174
Meatballs 164
Meatball Stew 225
Steak with Tomatoes (alla Pizzaiola) 233

Pasta
Baker's Pasta 94
Farmer's Pasta 88
Lasagne alla Paterna 90
Pasta Pie 43
Pasta with Beans 228
Pasta with Cauliflower 226
Pasta with Lentils 227

Rice Balls 58

Sauces
Christmas Day Gravy 171
Marinara 167
Meat 167
Octopus 143
Tomato 167

Sausage
Sausage and Peppers 108
Sausage Pie (Casatiello) 208
Sausage, Roasted with Potatoes
 and Peppers 95

Vegetables
Artichokes, Stuffed 187
Asparagus, Breaded 219
Cherry Peppers, Stuffed 188
Eggplant, Marinated 188
Eggplant Parmigiana 104
Eggplant, Stuffed 114
Escarole, Stuffed 148
Mushroom and Dried Sausage 212
Peppers and Potato Salad 234
Peppers, Roasted with Pine Nuts 213
Peppers, Roasted with Sun-Dried
 Tomatoes 98
String Beans in Sauce 229
Tomatoes, Stuffed 111
Vegetable Stew (Ciambotta) 236
Zucchini, Grilled with Mint 235

The Feast of the Seven Fishes:
A Brooklyn Italian's Recipes
Celebrating Food & Family
Photographs © 2019 Daniel Paterna Text © 2019
Daniel Paterna
Preface © 2019 Michael Lomonaco

All rights reserved. No part of this book may
be reproduced in any manner in any media, or
transmitted by any means whatsoever, electronic
or mechanical (including photocopy, film or
video recording, internet posting, or any other
information storage and retrieval system),
without the prior written permission of
the publisher.

Published in the United States
by powerHouse Books,
a division of powerHouse Cultural
Entertainment, Inc.
32 Adams Street, Brooklyn, NY 11201-1021
e-mail: info@powerHouseBooks.com
website: www.powerHouseBooks.com

First edition, 2019
Library of Congress Control Number: 2019944510
ISBN 978-1-57687-915-3

Design: Daniel Paterna

Printed and bound by EBS in Verona, Italiy
10 9 8 7 6 5 4 3 2 1